MRS v. Riverboat Queen
Case Files

MRS v. Riverboat Queen
Case Files

Cheryl Brown Wattley

NATIONAL INSTITUTE FOR TRIAL ADVOCACY

Address inquiries to:

Reprint Permission
National Institute for Trial Advocacy
1685 38th Street, Suite 200
Boulder, CO 80301-2735
Phone: (800) 225-6482
Fax: (720) 890-7069
E-mail: permissions@nita.org

ISBN 978-1-60156-336-1
FBA 1336

14 13 12 11 10 9 8 7 6 5 4 3 2 1

Printed in the United States of America

CONTENTS

1) MARINE RESCUE AND SALVAGE

v.

RIVERBOAT QUEEN

[Breach of Contract]

RIVERBOAT QUEEN

v.

MARINE RESCUE AND SALVAGE

[Counterclaim – Fraud and Misrepresentation]

---

2) RIVERBOAT QUEEN

v.

INSUR-ALL INSURANCE COMPANY

[Insurance: Bad Faith]

---

3) RIVERBOAT QUEEN

v.

NITA CITY

[Landlord/Tenant]

---

4) STATE OF NITA

v.

FRED GLENN

[Insurance Fraud]

FILE SUMMARY

This case file presents four lawsuits, one with a counterclaim. It also includes a criminal case as well as three civil cases—this increases the versatility of the file and allows it to be used for course exercises as well as the final trial. An instructor for a semester-long course can use these complementary case files in a variety of ways. For example, one or two of the civil lawsuits can be used as the problem through the instructional period. Then, the other lawsuits can be used for the final trial. This approach would require students to develop some new witness examinations and arguments for the final trial, but would not burden them with learning a completely new case file. Used in this manner, the students would not simply be repeating the exercises that they performed during the semester. At the same time, they would have a familiarity with the facts that would allow them to focus on case presentation and advocacy skills.

The scenario underlying the cases involves The Riverboat Queen, an entertainment paddleboat that mysteriously sank. It was owned and operated by Fred Glenn. Glenn had insurance coverage on the Riverboat Queen through Insur-All Insurance Company, but the policy was due to expire three days after the boat sank. The insurance company was requiring a full inspection of the boat before the company would renew the policy. After the boat sank, Glenn hired Marine Rescue and Salvage to raise the Riverboat Queen from the bottom of the lake and tow it to the shore. The Riverboat Queen had been docked at and operated from a boat ramp leased from Nita City. The lease contained a provision that the city could terminate the lease if it developed evidence that Glenn had violated any laws.

The cases included in this file are:

1. *Marine Rescue and Salvage (MRS) v. Fred Glenn, dba Riverboat Queen* [Breach of Contract]

   Fred Glenn dba Riverboat Queen v. Marine Rescue and Salvage (MRS)

   [Counterclaim—Fraud and Misrepresentation]

These cases revolve around the contract dispute between Fred Glenn and MRS. Mr. Glenn asserts an affirmative defense and counterclaim that MRS secured the contract by fraud and deception. The disputes are described as follows:

a) There is a dispute as to compensation, if any, due to MRS. The contract recites a price of $75,000 for services in raising the sunken boat. The contract contains three specific clauses that are the subject of the litigation: 1) a "No Cure, No Pay" clause; 2) a "Promise of Co-operation Clause; and 3) a special equipment clause. All of the e-mails and correspondence leading to the execution of the contract stated that MRS would provide all equipment. MRS rented equipment in its efforts to raise and remove the boat. Was there a "meeting of the minds" as to whether the costs for the rental of that equipment would be borne by the Riverboat Queen? What is the effect of the "No Cure, No Pay" and "Promise of Co-operation" clauses?

b) Not all of the contract paragraphs are initialed by Fred Glenn. Was there an agreement on paragraphs that were not initialed?

c) Was the MRS contract terminated? The contract does not provide any date by which MRS must end its efforts to raise the boat. After ninety days, MRS had not been able to remove the boat from the lake. The owner of the boat confronted MRS about the lack of success and threatened to bring in another company. MRS walked off the job claiming that the letter fired them and that the owner terminated the contract. In the absence of an express provision in the contract, a standard of "reasonable length of time" applies. Did the owner terminate the contract by writing the letter or did MRS terminate the contract by walking off the job? If the letter terminated MRS, was more than ninety days a "reasonable length of time" to allow MRS to try and raise the boat, such that the Fred Glenn could lawfully terminate the contract?

2. *Fred Glenn dba The Riverboat Queen v. Insur-All Insurance Company*: [Bad Faith Denial of an Insurance Claim; Breach of Contract.]

This case presents the issue of whether Insur-All's denial of Glenn's claim was in good faith or was it done in bad faith, allowing MRS to receive treble damages? The dispute is described as follows:

a) The insurance contract with Insur-All Insurance Company insured the hull of the boat for $500,000. The insurance company usually requires an inspection of the boat before a policy is issued. Insur-All Insurance Company did not require an inspection of the Riverboat Queen; it issued the policy without one. The boat sank three days before the expiration of the insurance policy. Glenn was notified that his insurance would not be renewed unless the company received an inspection report. The boat sank within days of Glenn receiving this notice. The insurance company denied the claim on alternative bases that 1) the boat had not been properly maintained as required under the policy; and/or 2)Glenn intentionally sank the boat.

3. *Fred Glenn dba The Riverboat Queen v. Nita City*: [Breach of Contract: Landlord/Tenant.]

This case is based on Glenn's lease with Nita City for the boat dock. The dispute is described as follows:

a) Glenn had a contract with Nita City to rent the boat dock. The lease contained a provision that Glenn maintain insurance. There was also a provision that allowed for the termination of the lease if the city reasonably believed that Glenn had "engaged in unlawful activity." The city invoked both provisions in terminating the lease. Was there proper cause to terminate the lease based on those clauses?

4. *State of Nita v. Fred Glenn*: [Water Hazard Act (pollution); Attempted Insurance Fraud.]

This is a state criminal prosecution of Glenn. The dispute is described as follows:

a) The state of Nita has brought a prosecution against Fred Glenn, charging him with a violation of the Nita Water Hazard Act and attempted insurance fraud. The State alleges that Glenn deliberately sank the Riverboat Queen, which "recklessly caused a condition that could lead to the discharge of pollutants into the waters of the State." The state also alleges that Glenn attempted to commit insurance fraud by submitting a claim to Insur-All Insurance Company.

WITNESSES:

1. Dolly Keith, owner of Marine Rescue and Salvage
2. Brad Keith, Dolly's son and co-owner of Marine Rescue and Salvage
3. Rick Smart, Captain of the recovery team for Marine Rescue and Salvage
4. Fred Glenn, Owner/builder of the Riverboat Queen
5. Jerry Williams, Maintenance man for the Riverboat Queen
6. Rocky Roberts, Mobile Environmental Co. employee
7. Linda Murchison, Employee of Nita City
8. Bob Richardson, Insurance company claims adjustor
9. Scott Gardner, Nita City Manager
10. Steve Palmer, Boat inspector
11. Barbara Campbell, Nita City employee

MARINE RESCUE AND SALVAGE V. RIVERBOAT QUEEN; RIVERBOAT QUEEN V. MARINE RESCUE AND SALVAGE

Marine Rescue Witnesses

Dolly Keith

Brad Keith

Rick Smart

Riverboat Queen Witnesses

Fred Glenn

Jerry Williams

Rocky Roberts

Riverboat Queen v. Insur-All Insurance Company [Insurance Fraud]

Riverboat Queen Witnesses

Fred Glenn

Steve Palmer

Rocky Roberts

Insur-all Insurance Company Witnesses

Bob Richardson

Dolly Keith

Rick Smart

Riverboat Queen v. Nita City [Landlord/Tenant]

Riverboat Queen Witnesses

Fred Glenn

Jerry Williams

Barbara Campbell

Nita City Witnesses

Linda Murchison

Dolly Keith

Scott Gardner

State of Nita v. Fred Glenn [Insurance Fraud]

State of Nita Witnesses

Dolly Keith

Bob Richardson

Linda Murchison

Rick Smart

Defense Witnesses

Fred Glenn

Jerry Williams

Rocky Roberts

Steve Palmer

STATEMENT OF THE CASE

MARINE RESCUE AND SALVAGE V. FRED GLENN DBA
THE RIVERBOAT QUEEN

The Riverboat Queen was an authentic paddleboat that sank for unknown reasons in a recreational lake in Darrow County on June 14, YR-2. Marine Rescue and Salvage (MRS) competed for a bid to raise the boat and remove it from the lake. After negotiations, a contract was entered into between Fred Glenn, the builder and owner of The Riverboat Queen, and Dolly Keith (Keith), one of the owners of MRS.

MRS began operations to raise the boat on July 2, YR-2. The captain of the recovery team was Rick Smart, a former navy salvage specialist. The MRS recovery team also included Brad Keith (Dolly's son), a certified scuba diver who had worked for a marine salvage company in Galveston, Texas; Gus Wilson, a tender; and Ryan Jones, the back-up diver.

While Keith was at the lake working to raise The Riverboat Queen, she became friends with Linda Murchison, the Nita City employee responsible for lake management. As Keith became frustrated in her efforts to raise the boat, she began talking with Murchison, continuously complaining about Glenn. After ninety days, The Riverboat Queen was still on the bottom of the lake.

Glenn was concerned that it was taking too long to raise the boat. Because the boat operated on diesel engines and used hydraulic fluids as part of its steering system, the potential for environmental hazard existed every day that the boat remained in the water. On the day that the boat sank, Nita City brought in an environmental containment company, Mobile Environmental Co., to contain any possible fuel leaks. As long as there was a threat of a fuel leak, Mobile Environmental Co. had to be present any time work was being done. Mobile Environmental Co., at the direction of Linda Murchison, was billing Glenn at the rate of $1,000 per day for the duration of time the boat was in the water.

On October 25, YR-2, Glenn wrote a letter to MRS. Upon receipt of that letter MRS declared it to be a termination letter, ceased work on the boat, packed up all of its equipment, and left the job site. Dolly Keith was very upset. MRS had spent a lot of money on the job. It had bought new equipment and paid the dive team. The company had spent considerable money during the ninety (90) days. Keith vowed that she would get even with Glenn.

Keith called Murchison and told her that Glenn had fired MRS. She told her that MRS had not been paid for any of the work that they had done. Keith also told Murchison that she suspected that Glenn fired them because Glenn was afraid that MRS would discover that he had actually sunk the boat for the insurance money.

After MRS walked off the job, Glenn hired Mobile Environmental Co. to get the Riverboat Queen out of the lake. Mobile Environmental Co. brought in bulldozers and other equipment to attach to the Riverboat Queen and pull it out of the lake.

It took several days, but Mobile Environmental Co. was able to pull the boat out of the lake. Five days after the boat was brought to shore, Glenn filed a claim with Insur-All. The insurance company denied the claim on the alternative bases that the boat had not been properly maintained and/or that Glenn had caused the boat to sink.

STATEMENT OF THE CASE

FRED GLENN DBA THE RIVERBOAT QUEEN V. INSUR-ALL INSURANCE COMPANY

After the Riverboat Queen sank, Glenn gave notice to Insur-All Insurance Company of the sinking so that it would be aware of the potential claim. Glenn's insurance policy was due to expire in three days. About thirty days before the boat sank, Glen had received a letter from Insur-All about the renewal of the policy. Insur-All told him that before it would renew the policy, it would have to receive a full inspection report. Under the lease with Nita City, Glenn had to have insurance on the boat to operate it and to keep it at the city dock. Without insurance, Glenn would have to close his business, move his boat, and be liable for the monthly docking fees.

An Insur-All's claims adjustor, Bob Richardson, reviewed Glenn's claim. He interviewed Dolly Keith and Linda Murchison. He asked Glenn to produce all records relating to the construction and maintenance of the boat, but no such records were ever delivered. After his investigation, Richardson determined that the claim should be denied.

STATEMENT OF THE CASE

FRED GLENN DBA THE RIVERBOAT QUEEN V. NITA CITY

Glenn dba The Riverboat Queen had a lease agreement with Nita City to dock the boat at the public boat ramp. This was an important lease because it was the only dock on the lake that was large enough to be used by the Riverboat Queen or any entertainment-type boat. It was important that the dock extend far enough out into the lake, away from the shoreline, for the water to be deep enough for the boat to dock.

When the boat sank, Glenn called Linda Murchison and told her that the Riverboat Queen had sunk, but Murchison had already been notified. Murchison had received a call from the Nita park service about the boat. She had called Mobile Environmental Co. to set booms to keep any boat fluids from leaking into the lake. Nita City invoked two provisions to terminate the lease: 1) that Glenn had to have insurance; and 2) that the lease could be terminated on reasonable belief that Glenn was engaging, or had engaged, in unlawful conduct.

STATEMENT OF THE CASE

STATE OF NITA V. FRED GLENN

The State of Nita has charged Fred Glenn with two criminal offenses: 1) violation of the Nita Water Hazards Act; and 2) attempted insurance fraud. The Water Hazards Act prohibits the creation of any condition that leads, or could lead, to the discharge of pollutants in the state water resources. It is alleged that Glenn recklessly caused the sinking of the boat, which created a condition that could lead to discharge of pollutants into the lake. The state also charges that Glenn attempted to commit insurance fraud by submitting a claim to Insur-All Insurance Company. Glenn has entered a plea of not guilty and the case is set for jury trial.

DEPOSITION OF DOLLY KEITH

1 My son, Brad, is a certified diver and has worked for a boat salvage company for several
2 years. Like many young men, my son wanted to become his own boss. Fortunately, I had
3 the financial resources to purchase a boat recovery company and open such a business
4 with my son. We bought the assets and customer list of another company and then named
5 it "Marine Rescue and Salvage." I had never been involved in the boat recovery business,
6 but I had owned several other enterprises before, including a neighborhood gas station,
7 a plant shop, and a bookstore. With all of these other businesses, I would own them for a
8 couple of years and then sell them for a profit.
9
10 We bought MRS in YR-4. Brad was so excited. I remember the afternoon that we signed
11 the purchase documents. After we signed, we went to the lot where all of the equipment
12 was stored. Even though we had the inventory of the equipment, we looked at each piece,
13 each item as if we'd never seen it before. There was a pontoon boat, a rowboat, a camper,
14 ten scuba tanks, and five neoprene wet suits, and other items.
15
16 We did a variety of marine work. Brad would clean boat hulls, do inspection work, and
17 raise sunken boats. We didn't make a lot of money, but we did make $10,000 to $15,000
18 a year in profit. Not to mention that both Brad and I were paid salaries of $35,000 a year.
19
20 On June 14, YR-2, I got a call from Fred Glenn. Rocky Roberts had referred him to us. We
21 knew Rocky because he had been the environmental specialist on one of the sites where
22 we had raised a sunken boat. Mr. Glenn described his boat, said that it had sunk, and said
23 he needed to get it raised and removed from the lake. We had never worked on a boat that
24 big, but the principles in raising a boat are the same whether it is small or big.
25
26 We talked a couple of times. He was very pleasant and business-like. He sent me e-mails
27 with questions, and I answered them. I told him that I thought that we could get the boat
28 out even though we had never worked on a boat that big. I told him that I would charge
29 him $75,000 to get the boat out of the lake. That was just our base fee given the size of the
30 boat. I knew that our contract had additional provisions for equipment rental and special
31 circumstances. We have to have that type of provision because you can't predict all of the
32 equipment that you will need until you are on the job. I always told Mr. Glenn that we had
33 a standard contract that set out all of the charges and that you could never anticipate all
34 of the problems that could come up.
35
36 Our contract has a "No Cure, No Pay" provision that is fairly standard. If we don't get the
37 boat up, we don't get paid. But we have always been successful in raising the boat.
38
39 We also have a "Promise of Cooperation" clause in our contract. This provision is very
40 important to us because we have to have the owner's assistance to get information such as
41 measurements, weights, equipment location and distances. This is particularly important
42 because we have to get that information to raise the boat. Also, if there are defects or

1   problems with the boat that aren't disclosed to us, they could be a safety hazard as well
2   as keeping us from getting the boat up, which means we wouldn't get paid.
3
4   Glenn signed a contract for MRS to raise the Riverboat Queen. The contract clearly says he
5   is to pay for any equipment that we have to rent or purchase. I don't know why Glenn didn't
6   initial that paragraph. He never said that he wasn't going to pay for the equipment rental.
7
8   We started work on raising the boat on July 2, YR-2. Our plan was to pump water out of
9   the interior of the boat to reduce the weight. Then we would put straps under the boat to
10 be attached to flotation bags. We would attach the flotation bags to the straps, inflate the
11 flotation bags and the boat would literally float up.
12
13 From the beginning it was a disaster. Glenn couldn't, or wouldn't, tell us where all of the
14 doors and windows were so that we could board them up. We kept finding something
15 else that needed to be boarded up—it took over a week just to get the boards up. Then
16 Glenn wanted to control where we cut the holes to put the pumps that would pump the
17 water out of the boat. It was a real problem because we were trying to avoid the gas tanks
18 and the hydraulic holding tanks. The tanks were pretty full, and I was concerned about
19 causing any holes and leaks. We had figured out the safest places to put the pumps, but
20 he refused to let us cut there. He was constantly making us change our plans, interfering
21 with my crew, making it really difficult for us to work. Looking back, it was like he had
22 something to hide.
23
24 We were never able to keep water from flowing into the boat. We would pump water out
25 of the boat during the day, but the next morning the water level would be up again. We
26 had painted a line on the side of the boat and it would go up as the water level went down
27 because the boat was getting lighter. But, when we'd come in in the morning, the line
28 would be at water level again because the boat had taken on water. It was as if someone
29 was pumping water into the boat at night while we were gone.
30
31 By this time, several weeks had passed. Glenn started trying to get me to use bulldozers
32 to just drag the boat out. I kept telling him that using bulldozers would put too much
33 stress on the boat and would cause it to break apart. I also told him that dragging the boat
34 along the bottom of the lake would cause more damage and tear up the hull. I also said
35 that if the boat was torn up, he might "never know what caused it to sink." He said that "if
36 that happens, so be it, I'll be OK." I didn't ask what he meant by that, but I assumed that
37 he was referring to an insurance payment and that he would be OK financially.
38
39 I finally decided that we had to reduce the weight of the boat. We had to cut off some of
40 the metal parts. I mean the boat weighed over 300,000 pounds—it was made of steel!
41 We needed to cut off the top deck because that weighed about 100,000 pounds. It would
42 make it easier for the flotation bags.
43
44 When I explained the process to Glenn, he was really reluctant to agree. He said "just
45 drag it out with bulldozers." It took me a couple of days to get him to agree. It was really a

1   struggle. Once he agreed, however, he suddenly suggested that we should get the salvage
2   value because we were cutting up the metal. We would stack up the metal that we cut off
3   of the boat and then take it to the scrap metal yard.
4
5   Glenn finally stopped interfering. My crew and I started cutting the metal off. We even had
6   to order special cutting torches to be used to remove the metal. We were doing everything
7   that needed to be done to be able to raise the boat. It looked like we were really going to
8   succeed. The boat was getting lighter and the flotation devices were going to work.
9
10 Then, out of the blue, I got an e-mail from Glenn telling me that I needed to immediately
11 stop everything and not do any more work. He was firing me. That's all there is to it. He
12 told me not to go back to the lake. How were we supposed to get the boat up if we couldn't
13 go back to the lake?
14
15 I think that Glenn was afraid that we were going to figure out why the water level wasn't
16 staying down when we were pumping the water out. Water had to be coming in from
17 somewhere. If there was a hole, it was certain that we would find it as we kept cutting
18 the boat. But using bulldozers to pull the boat out would put such strain on the sides of
19 the boat that the boat would pull apart, making it impossible to tell whether there was an
20 earlier hole. The bulldozers would cover up what Glenn had done. Glenn realized that he
21 needed to do something to hide the evidence that he sunk the boat.
22
23 The day Glenn fired me, I went to Linda Murchison. She works for Nita City, which owns
24 the land where the boat was docked. I had gotten to know her while we were working
25 on the boat. She'd come out and visit, see how the job was progressing, and make sure
26 that there weren't any environmental problems. She saw how Glenn was constantly
27 interfering with what we were doing, and how he was keeping us from working.
28
29 I told Linda of my suspicions that Glenn had deliberately sunk the boat. I told her that
30 I had heard Glenn complaining about all of the medical bills he had for his wife and how
31 much debt there was. She didn't say so, but I think that she agreed with me. She asked me
32 to write up what I had seen about the boat and Glenn. She said that the City would not
33 want to be any part of anyone perpetrating a fraud and that they might have to terminate
34 his lease.
35
36 We put a lot of time into that job and rented a lot of equipment. If Glenn hadn't
37 interfered, I would have been able to make money on the $75,000 fee. But because of
38 his interference, I ran into overages for my crew. That cost me about $100,000. The
39 purchase of the special cutting torch and the rental of additional supplies such as
40 plywood to board up the doors and windows, extra scuba tanks because our guys had
41 to dive so long, oxygen tanks to run the torches, and all sorts of extra equipment was
42 $17,500. When Glenn fired me, it hurt me financially. Because I didn't get the $75,000, I
43 didn't have the money necessary to continue the business. We didn't have the money to
44 fund other jobs. We had to close the business. Now both Brad and I are both out of work.
45 We haven't had any income for two years.

SUPPLEMENTAL STATEMENT
GLENN V. INSUR-ALL INSURANCE COMPANY

While I was trying to raise the Riverboat Queen, I was contacted by Bob Richardson from the insurance company. In fact, I spoke to him several times: twice in person and twice on the telephone.

The first time that I spoke with Richardson was a few days after we started work. I don't remember the actual date. He just showed up. I didn't know that he was coming. He came up to me and introduced himself as being the adjustor from the insurance company. He said that it was his job to determine whether the insurance should pay Mr. Glenn's claim. He told me that they were some unusual circumstances about Mr. Glenn's insurance and that they thought that the sinking of the boat was very suspicious. He said that they had told Glenn that it would be best to float the boat up so that they could determine why the boat had sunk. He asked me to please let him know if we came across anything that did not appear to be appropriate. It was clear from his tone of voice and attitude that he didn't think very highly of Glenn.

The second time that I spoke with Richardson was when I called him. I was getting really frustrated with Mr. Glenn continually interfering with our efforts to get the boat up. I was trying to figure out if Glenn's interference was somehow related to getting his insurance payment.

Richardson came out to the site sometime after that call. We were cutting the boat by then. I told him about my conversations with Glenn regarding the use of bulldozers to drag the boat out. I also told him that I had said dragging the boat out would probably destroy any evidence of what made the boat sink. I told him that Mr. Glenn said essentially, "So be it. I'll be fine anyway because they have to pay if they can't figure out what caused it to sink."

The last time that I spoke with Richardson was the day Glenn fired us. I called and told him what Glenn had done. I also told him that Glenn was going to use bulldozers to just drag the boat out of the lake. I also told him about Glenn's complaining about his wife's medical bills.

I haven't spoken to Richardson since then. Linda told me that Insur-All did not pay the claim.

SUPPLEMENTAL STATEMENT: GLENN V. NITA CITY

I never knew the specific provisions of the lease. Linda told me one day when she was at the lake that if Glenn had done something unlawful, she was going to get the lease terminated. She said something about Glenn having just renewed the lease, but that there was no way that she was going to let someone who had broken the law stay on the boat ramp for another five years. She talked a lot about the potential pollution of the lake. She

1   was really adamant about that. Sometimes Linda would get so agitated that it seemed
2   like it was personal, but I think that is because she cares about her job so much. She was
3   really upset because the fluids in the sunken boat threatened the water supply in the
4   lake. She was really stressed about that. She told me that she was up for a promotion
5   and that she didn't want anything to happen on this project that would make her look
6   bad. One time she made some remark about she'd get Glenn if he polluted the water
7   supply and put her promotion in jeopardy just to get some money because he couldn't
8   run his business and was having financial problems. But that was at the end of the day,
9   and I don't know whether she really meant it or not.
10
11 ## SUPPLEMENTAL STATEMENT: STATE OF NITA V. FRED GLENN
12
13
14 The sunken Riverboat Queen was a real pollution threat. The environmental booms were
15 placed around the boat. But even though we did our best, it always seemed that some
16 diesel fuel or hydraulic fluid was leaking into the lake. The tanks were almost full, so they
17 posed a real threat if punctured or ruptured. When any boat sinks, it is always hard to
18 contain the fluids, but the size of the Riverboat Queen makes it even more likely. From
19 the moment I stepped on to the boat until I stepped off, there was a risk of fluids seeping
20 from the boat.
21
22 When we first started working on raising the boat, Mr. Glenn and I got along really well.
23 He was very pleasant to talk with. But after a few days, he was like a totally different
24 person. He was rude, very obnoxious in his conversations. He'd cut off any explanations
25 that I was trying to give him; he seemed mad if I had a question to ask him. I sometimes
26 tried to excuse his behavior because I knew that he was under a lot of stress because of
27 his wife's illness. But his behavior was really uncalled for. When I proposed that we cut
28 off some of the metal to lighten the boat, I was surprised that he seemed reluctant to
29 follow that recommendation.
30
31 But a few days before he fired me, we had a really bad argument. Mr. Glenn was calling me
32 incompetent, saying that I didn't know what I was doing and that he should never have
33 made a deal with us. He said, "You are going to ruin everything; you're going to cause me
34 even bigger problems than I have now." At the time, I thought that was a really weird thing
35 to say. But looking back, I see now that Mr. Glenn was so agitated because we weren't
36 going to drag the boat out. Floating it up would have allowed an inspection to find the
37 hole(s) that caused the boat to sink. And there could have been a determination whether
38 the hole(s) had been intentionally created to cause the boat to sink. As far as I concerned,
39 that is what Mr. Glenn was afraid of and that's why he kept being rude. Things weren't
40 working out his way.

Deposition of Brad Keith

1   My name is Brad Keith. My mother and I own Marine Rescue and Salvage. I'm twenty-
2   six years old, and all of my life I have loved to swim. I was a lifeguard while I was in
3   high school. Then when I graduated from high school, I went down to the Gulf of Mexico
4   because I thought that I would try and get some work on one of the offshore drilling rigs
5   for a while. But when I got there, I found a job working for a marine salvage company.
6
7   The owner of that company, Russell Garner, took me under his wing and taught me the
8   business. Because he was on the gulf, he had all sorts of work. He did some big commercial
9   work with the offshore drilling rigs. Some of his divers would do underwater welding or
10   chain cutting to remove old oil rigs. Sometimes a ship might get grounded on a sand bar,
11   and Russell's company would be hired to refloat the boat. He did wreck removal service
12   for the Navy and Coast Guard. Then, sometimes, he would work on pleasure watercraft
13   such as speed boats, pontoon boats, and jet skis.
14
15   I worked with him for about four years. At first, I handled the customers, wrote up the
16   contracts, and generally served as Russell's assistant. When Russell would bid a job, he
17   would first go to the site of the wreck or grounded boat. He'd decide what approach to
18   take to get the boat up and then develop a plan for removing the boat. He would decide
19   how many divers were needed, what type of equipment would be used, and how many
20   flotation bags might be needed. Then he would write that up as a "Recovery Plan."
21
22   Russell would give me the recovery plan and the start date for the job. The recovery plan
23   would identify which divers he wanted for that job. I would contact the divers and set them
24   up on a work schedule based on the recovery plan. I would also have to "reserve" all of the
25   equipment so that it would be ready when it was time to start the job. We usually had the
26   equipment that was needed. I can't remember a time when we had to rent any equipment.
27
28   While I worked for Russell, I got certified as a scuba diver. I really wanted to start working
29   on some of the actual jobs. I did work on some the pleasure craft jobs, cleaning the hulls,
30   doing inspections. There was also one boat that I helped to refloat—it was a speed boat.
31   Towards the end of my time working for Russell, I began working on some of the larger
32   salvage jobs.
33
34   Then in YR-4, my mother heard about a boat recovery company that was for sale in Nita.
35   I had already decided that I wanted to move back to Nita so this sounded like a perfect
36   opportunity. I would be able to take all of the knowledge that I had gained working for
37   Russell and use it for my own company. On top of that, the guy that we were buying the
38   company from, Rick Smart, agreed to serve as a consultant for us.
39
40   Having Rick work as a consultant made sense. He was financing our purchase of the
41   company for $250,000 for ten years. We were paying $2,400 a month. By being our
42   consultant, Rick was helping us to earn money to make sure that he got his payment. With

1   this arrangement, it was in Rick's interest to make sure that our jobs were completed and
2   that we got paid. Because of all of the problems with the Riverboat Queen, Mom and I lost
3   Marine Recovery Specialists and never paid Rick all of his money.
4
5   When we bought MRS, we were real excited. We put together a Web site, a marketing
6   campaign, and a "coupon" program that we took around to marinas. We were pretty
7   aggressive in getting new business. Within just a couple of months, we were making
8   regular money doing hull cleanings and inspections. We were doing well—we never
9   missed a payment to Rick, and we took salaries.
10
11   When Mom was contacted by Mr. Glenn about the Riverboat Queen, I went out to Beacon
12   Lake to see the boat. Because the water was not very deep, the top deck of the boat
13   was not under water. I was able to go out to the boat and walk around that deck. I took
14   measurements of the boat, measured the depth of the water, and did a general inspection.
15   I stayed out there about an hour to look over things. Glenn wasn't there to answer any
16   questions, but that really didn't matter. I could see everything that I needed to know.
17   I could see where the fuel tanks and hydraulic pumps were.
18
19   When I got back to my office, I figured out a recovery plan for the boat. I had never been
20   totally responsible for a boat this size, but the principles for floating a boat are the same
21   regardless of size. You need to lighten the boat so that the flotation bags, which are
22   attached to the boat, can pull it up. Based on my recovery plan, Mom and I determined that
23   we could do the job for $75,000 and make a profit. We knew that our contract required
24   the boat owner to pay for any extra equipment that we needed to rent or buy. Our price
25   would have been higher if we had to pay for that extra equipment.
26
27   The job started out great. Ryan Jones and I were the lead divers. Gus Wilson served as a
28   "tender"—he monitored us while we were in the water and made sure that our air tanks
29   were ready. Some days we would have day divers we hired to help us out. Rick is a master
30   diver, so he was always available to help out if we needed more people in the water. Mom
31   could also serve as the "dive captain" to monitor the divers in the water.
32
33   The problem that we ran into was that Glenn couldn't, or wouldn't, tell us where all of
34   the doors and windows were. He had provided us with diagrams, but they weren't very
35   helpful. I mean when you are underwater and the visibility isn't great, you need actual
36   dimensions; you have to know how far apart things are. Each time we thought that we
37   had everything boarded up so that we could pump the water out, we'd find another place
38   where water was flowing in. It seemed like he was trying to sabotage us or something. He
39   sure wasn't helping. I mean, there was one section of the boat near the paddles that just
40   had chain link fencing covering the back engine room. He never told us that. Of course
41   water can flow into the back engine room through a chain link fence!
42
43   Then Mr. Glenn started complaining all the time. He would stand on the top deck while
44   we were trying to board things up, screaming at us. Every time we'd start working on a
45   new area, he'd insist that we surface and tell him what we had seen. It got ridiculous.

1   After a few weeks, Mom, Rick, and I decided that we needed to cut some of the top deck
2   to make the boat lighter. We had put out flotation devices and pumped water out of the
3   boat, but the boat wouldn't "break suction." That means that the boat is stuck in the mud
4   that was the bottom of the lake. Mom talked to Glenn about that. I don't know what he
5   said, I just know that we started cutting the boat.
6
7   Rick and I did the cutting. It's pretty dangerous to have too many people using cutting
8   torches at the same time. It was tedious work, but we were making pretty good progress.
9   We had to be careful how we cut the boat up because you don't want to weaken the
10   structure of the boat. You don't want the boat collapsing in on itself.
11
12   While we were working, Rocky Roberts and Glenn would be on the shore. You could tell
13   that they were talking; you could see them pointing at us, shaking their heads. Rocky was
14   really trying to get the job for his company. He told me one time that he got a commission
15   for each job that he brought to the company.
16
17   Then one day, Mr. Glenn told me that he wanted us to get bulldozers and just pull the Riverboat
18   Queen out of the lake. He said that he didn't care if the boat pulled apart. He said that it was
19   just a big piece of junk now anyways. I tried to tell him that the lower deck was still intact
20   and he would be able to repair what we had cut off. He didn't want to hear that. He wasn't
21   interested in how he could rebuild the boat. He just wanted us to drag it out with bulldozers.
22   "Do it and let's be done with this. I've got to get my insurance and get on with my life," he said.
23
24   When we didn't get the bulldozers like he wanted, Mr. Glenn fired us. We could have
25   finished the job. We would have refloated the Riverboat Queen to the shore just like we
26   were contracted to do. We were capable of doing the job. Mr. Glenn just kept interfering
27   and then fired us.
28
29   We lost our investment in MRS. Both my Mom and I are out of jobs. We spent over
30   $100,000 during the almost four months that we were out there working.
31
32
33   ## SUPPLEMENTAL STATEMENT:
34   ## GLENN V. INSUR-ALL INSURANCE COMPANY
35
36   I met Bob Richardson when he came out to the boat shortly after we started working.
37   He asked me to explain to him what we were doing to raise the boat. He seemed to agree
38   with our approach. He was very interested in my assessment of the boat's condition.
39   I remember telling him that overall I was surprised that the boat had ever floated. There
40   were all sorts of hoses and wires running all over the place without any apparent function.
41   I told him that I had really been surprised at how little Glenn seemed to know about his
42   boat. I mean, he built it, but then he couldn't tell us where the windows, doors, and other
43   openings were when we were trying to block all spaces where water could be flowing
44   in. I also told him how Glenn kept interfering with the divers. Richardson seemed really
45   interested in that; he even took notes while we were talking.

SUPPLEMENTAL STATEMENT: GLENN V. NITA CITY

Linda Murchison was out at the boat a lot while we working on it. She was really concerned about the potential of fluids leaking into the water supply. A couple of times I heard her talking on the phone, saying that if she could find any way to get rid of Fred Glenn and terminate his lease, she would do it. She said that "she was sick of him," that "he needed to go." I remember that because I thought that it was very unprofessional of her. She was almost yelling.

I kept reassuring her that we had it under control and that Mobile Environmental Co. was there if there should be an accidental spillage. I couldn't understand why she was so intense.

SUPPLEMENTAL STATEMENT: STATE OF NITA V. FRED GLENN

I spent more time around the Riverboat Queen than anyone else after it sank. I am the person who swam underwater, running my hands alongside the hull of the boat looking for the holes in the boat. The windows were all knocked out. The doors were gone. It doesn't make sense that all of the windows and doors were gone. If the Riverboat Queen had sunk normally, the water would have come in from the bottom and it would have taken some time to fill the boat and there would not have been any pressure to cause the windows and doors to pop out. With the windows and doors knocked out, when the boat began to sink it would quickly fill with water and go to the bottom of the lake. It would also make it harder to bring it up.

The fuel tanks are on the side of the boat. They look like white rectangular boxes. We were always struggling to make certain that the fuel caps were not leaking and that there was not seepage into the lake.

DEPOSITION OF RICK SMART

1   I began Marine Rescue and Salvage after I got out of the Navy. I had owned it for
2   twenty years before I sold it to the Keiths. I was getting ready for retirement, and selling
3   them the company while still keeping my hand in it by being a consultant seemed ideal.
4
5   I was about twenty when I dropped out of college and joined the Navy. That may be part
6   of the reason that I wanted to sell to Brad—I could remember when I was that age and
7   excited about diving and salvage work. That's what I did in the Navy, diving and salvage.
8   I attended the training program in Panama City, Florida. After basic scuba training, I took
9   some of the advanced courses in underwater cutting and welding procedures. We also
10   had simulation training for salvage and boat recovery.
11
12   I spent four years in the Navy. Almost all of my duty time was spent on salvage teams. We
13   rescued downed helicopters, tugboats, barges, and Coast Guard vessels. I worked on just
14   about every type of ship.
15
16   Obviously, when I came back to Nita City, I knew that I wouldn't be working on those big,
17   commercial ships anymore. But I decided to set up Marine Rescue and Salvage because
18   there are a lot of pleasure craft on Beacon Lake. After a while, I was able to build up a
19   pretty good business because I would travel to other states as well to do salvage work.
20   I developed contacts with divers in a number of states, using my Navy contacts, so that
21   I had the manpower to get the work done.
22
23   Dolly and Brad bid on the Riverboat Queen job without talking to me. I was out of town
24   on vacation, and I guess Mr. Glenn was in a pretty big hurry. Anyway, when I got back
25   into town, Dolly told me about the job. Brad had written up a "recovery plan," which is
26   pretty standard in the business. I looked over the plan, and it seemed to be pretty basic.
27   Of course, I hadn't seen the boat or the specific area of the lake where it had sunk.
28
29   When we got out to the lake that first morning, I did my own inspection from the top
30   deck. Everything seemed to be fine. Brad had done a good job of getting measurements.
31   We just had to pump the water out of the boat, attach the flotation bags, and float the boat
32   up. It should have been a fairly straightforward job even if it was a big boat.
33
34   I didn't review the contract that Glenn signed. Usually, Dolly would have me look over
35   new contracts, and we would talk about them to make sure that the job was going to be
36   profitable. Because I was out of town, I never looked at this contract.
37
38   One of the first things that Brad and I did when we got out to the lake was to take a
39   survey of the boat. The divers, Brad and Ryan, swam around the boat trying to feel
40   the hull and see if they could find out where the hole was that caused the boat to sink.
41   That's another thing that is very fundamental—find out where the water is going into
42   the boat. But what they did find that was really unusual is that all of the windows and

1 doors were knocked out. That was really going to interfere with pumping the water out.
2 We had to block those openings.
3
4 Initially, the divers didn't find any holes in the hull itself. But that didn't really bother me.
5 The boat was fairly large, of course. It wasn't as big as some of the boats that I had worked
6 on when I was in the Navy, but it was bigger than the pleasure craft that the Keiths had
7 usually worked on. When you're swimming underwater, particularly in that lake, you
8 don't have much visibility, so you rub your hand against the side of the boat looking for
9 any breaches in the hull. Because the hull was so big, I can understand why they didn't
10 find any holes. But there had to be a hole in the hull to let the water in below the windows
11 and door and to sink the boat. That is also pretty elementary.
12
13 I don't think that we were even out there working two days before Mr. Glenn started
14 interfering with what we were doing. Every time we sent the divers down, he'd start
15 making demands. He didn't want us to work that side of the boat. He wanted to know
16 what the divers were doing. He didn't want us to empty the fuel from the fuel tanks. He
17 was really being obstructive. I remember thinking one day, "Why did you hire us if you
18 don't want us to do our job?" In fact, at that point, I started wondering if he was trying
19 to hide something. He didn't want us to just float that boat up—if we had done that, we
20 would have been able to do a thorough examination of the hull and would have found the
21 hole(s) that caused the boat to start sinking.
22
23 When we weren't successful lifting the boat with the flotation devices, I recommended that
24 we reduce the weight of the boat by cutting off the smokestacks, railing, and top flooring.
25 We couldn't get the water pumped out, so we needed to lighten the boat another way.
26
27 Well, Glenn got really angry. He started yelling at Dolly that we should just get bulldozers
28 and drag it out. I couldn't figure that out. When we started Mr. Glenn was always talking
29 about wanting to fix the boat once it was recovered. Now, even though we told him that
30 dragging the boat would destroy it, he was yelling at us to get bulldozers. It didn't make
31 any sense.
32
33 But Dolly was sticking to the recovery plan. She was worried that if you used bulldozers
34 to just drag the boat out that the boat might split in half or other damage, including fuel
35 spills, could happen. We knew that water was still getting into the boat from somewhere.
36 When we got the pumps going and pumped the water out of the boat, the boat didn't get
37 lighter. That means that there was water flowing into the boat about as fast as we were
38 pumping it out. If water was flowing into the boat that fast, there had to be splits in the
39 sides of the boat where it had been welded together. Using bulldozers would put a strain
40 on those welds on the side and the boat would split. If that happened, the hydraulic fluid
41 and diesel fuel would spill into the water. Spilling those fluids into the city's water supply
42 would have been a catastrophe. But Mr. Glenn didn't care about that.
43
44 Then one day, Dolly gets a letter from Mr. Glenn telling us to get off of the property. He
45 told us to stop what we were doing, so we did. We'd been fired; there wasn't anything else

1 for us to do. We had put in a lot of time and into cutting the boat to make it lighter. I know
2 that it was a slow, tedious process, but it was the most conservative approach to take.
3
4 ## SUPPLEMENTAL STATEMENT:
5 ## GLENN V. INSUR-ALL INSURANCE COMPANY
6
7
8 I did not have much direct contact with the guy from the insurance company. I remember
9 that he came to the site one day. He introduced himself, but I don't remember his name.
10 He said that he was the person who would decide whether the insurance would pay
11 Mr. Glenn's claim. He asked a lot of questions. He told us that when we found something
12 suspicious to let him know. That struck me—it wasn't *if* we found something suspicious
13 or unusual, but *when*. It was like he knew that there was something wrong.
14
15 After that visit, I remembered a conversation that I had had with Mr. Glenn. This was
16 really early on in the project, probably during the first couple of weeks. Mr. Glenn and
17 I were just talking; the guys were in the lake attaching the flotation bags to the boat.
18 Mr. Glenn told me that he was glad that we were going to float the boat up. He said that
19 he didn't believe that the welds would hold the boat together if we were to drag it out. He
20 said that dragging the boat would probably damage it so badly that he would not be able
21 to fix it and use it again or find out what made it sink in the first place.
22
23 ## SUPPLEMENTAL STATEMENT: GLENN V. NITA CITY
24
25
26 Linda Murchison was out at the boat at lot. She was clearly concerned about what we
27 were doing. She and Dolly would talk quite a bit. A few times, she came over and asked
28 me some questions. One day we were talking about working for the government and
29 supervisors. She told me that she was up for a promotion and that the outcome of this
30 project would be a big part of that promotion decision. She said that the city manager
31 was a real stickler for following all the rules. She said that he had gone over each lease
32 with her, talked about all of the conditions for the leases, and made it clear to her that
33 those conditions should be strictly enforced. In fact, she quoted him as saying, "Every
34 decision you make should be in the city's best interest." I remember that because she
35 kind of made it a joke, calling herself the "lease police." She said that she could pretty
36 much do anything she wanted to do with the lease and that Fred Glenn better stay on her
37 "good side." We both laughed at that.
38
39 ## SUPPLEMENTAL STATEMENT: STATE OF NITA V. FRED GLENN
40
41
42 The first few days that we worked on raising the boat, Glenn talked with me a lot. He seemed
43 to be very interested in the work that I had done in the Navy, the types of boats that I had
44 worked on, the ways that you can tell what caused a boat to sink. He had a lot of questions.
45 I especially remember he asked about the tests and examinations that are made on boats

1   once they are raised to figure out why they sank. He made the bizarre comment, "Well, a hole
2   is a hole."
3
4   I didn't think much about that comment at the time, but right after that conversation,
5   Mr. Glenn started telling us to just drag the boat out, that he didn't care what happened
6   to it. One time, we had a really heated argument. He yelled at me to "just pull it out; I'm
7   paying you, do it my way." He was really irate, saying that he was under a lot of pressure
8   and that I didn't understand the big picture. In fact, that was something he said several
9   times, that "you don't understand the big picture."

Deposition of Fred Glenn

1   About fifteen years ago, my wife Elizabeth and I went to New Orleans. We went to dinner
2   on a riverboat. I was fascinated by the boat. Elizabeth and I walked around. The restaurant
3   was in an enclosed part of the boat, but there was an upper deck that was open. I loved
4   being on the water and standing on that deck.
5
6   My wife and I talked about the evening for quite some time. We decided that it would be a
7   great business opportunity to operate a restaurant on a boat on Beacon Lake. I've always
8   been a builder. I do welding. So Elizabeth and I started taking trips and traveling to every
9   paddle boat that we could find. I would talk to the captains, find out about their boats,
10 how the boats steered, what types of engines they had, all sorts of things. After about six
11 months we decided to do it: I would build a paddle boat.
12
13 I made my own blue prints. They were really just diagrams, but they worked for me.
14 I actually drew some similar diagrams and gave them to Brad Keith to help him with
15 bringing the boat up. I built the boat in my workshop on my farm. The Riverboat Queen
16 was 115 feet long, 36 feet wide. The front part of the boat had an engine that powered two
17 small propellers that moved the boat from side to side. This is also where the hydraulic
18 fluid was located. The back end of the boat had another engine that operated the paddles
19 that propelled the boat forward.
20
21 It was a double-decked boat. The bottom deck was enclosed, air conditioned, and heated.
22 In that downstairs area we had a commercial kitchen, a commercial refrigerator, grills—
23 the equipment that you see in a restaurant. We could seat about 150 people downstairs
24 for dinner.
25
26 The upper deck was shaded by a canopy, but other than that it was completely open. We
27 had chairs and tables, a full bar, and a music station. It was really fun to sit on the top deck
28 when we were cruising. We would do Fourth of July cruises, and it was always a great way
29 to watch the fireworks.
30
31 It took me four years to build the boat, working almost every day. I'll never forget the day
32 that we launched it. Once we got the boat in the water, we started up the paddles, put
33 them in reverse, and pulled the boat out into the water. It was such a great day. Knowing
34 that I had built that boat and seeing it turn from an idea into a plan and finally into a
35 reality was such a tremendous feeling. That boat has always meant a lot to me.
36
37 Running the boat as a business was hard work, even harder work than building it. We
38 would host weddings, birthday parties, anniversaries, school reunions, proms—all sorts
39 of events. It took both Elizabeth and I to advertise the boat, letting people know that we
40 were out there and could host their parties. But the business grew, and we began to build
41 a reputation and make a profit.

1   We then advertised for a chef. It took several months, but we got a creole chef from New
2   Orleans. It was great—New Orleans food on a New Orleans style riverboat, right in the
3   heart of Nita City!
4
5   The wheelhouse was on the top deck. That's where I would pilot the boat from. I had
6   a large, wooden, steering wheel. I kept it shiny and polished. I would stand in that
7   wheelhouse, look out over the water, listen to our passengers laughing and having a good
8   time—life was great.
9
10   Then, one day, June 14, YR-2, we got a telephone call. The Riverboat Queen had been
11   found on the bottom of the lake—she had sunk. My heart sunk too when I heard the
12   news. The boat was our business and our livelihood—I had built it with my own hands.
13
14   Even though I was quite upset when I heard the news, I knew that I had to respond to the
15   situation. I contacted the Nita water department to make certain that an environmental
16   company was on site to protect against any fuel spills. A fuel spill would be a real problem
17   because Beacon Lake is the water supply for Nita. Then I contacted my insurance company.
18   Later that day, I started contacting boat recovery companies to find someone who could
19   raise the boat. I thought that these were things that a responsible owner would do. And
20   I wanted to get the boat up as quickly as possible to see whether it could be saved and
21   repaired. It was really important to me to try to save my boat. The lake isn't very deep so
22   that the top deck of the boat was still above the water.
23
24   After I made those phone calls I went out to the lake to see the boat for myself. There are no
25   words to explain how I felt. But at the same time, I was hoping that we could save the boat.
26
27   I received bids to raise the boat. I decided that I would hire Marine Rescue and Salvage.
28   They had the best bid, but my selection was based on the customer service they gave.
29   Dolly Keith returned my initial phone call within an hour. She asked what seemed to be
30   good questions. She described the process that they would use and the equipment they
31   would require. I told her that I needed to get it done as quickly as possible, that I wanted to
32   get the boat up and try to save it, and that I was concerned that there could be a fuel spill.
33   She reassured me that they could get it done quickly and that I might be able to save my
34   boat. It sounded like she knew what she was talking about. She kept telling me, "This is the
35   kind of thing that we do." She made me believe that they had the manpower, equipment,
36   and experience to do the job. We talked over a couple of days and sent e-mails back and
37   forth working out the details of the deal. I didn't specifically ask her if they had ever raised
38   a boat 110 feet long, but I did tell her the boat's dimensions and she didn't say anything.
39
40   On the morning MRS started, I signed a contract. Dolly said that it was a form contract
41   that they always use and some of it didn't apply to our deal and that I didn't need to worry
42   about the paragraphs that didn't apply, I could just ignore them. I made sure that there
43   was a "no cure, no pay" provision. That's pretty standard in the boat recovery business.
44   I didn't have to pay MRS if they didn't bring the boat up and bring it ashore. If MRS was
45   successful, I would pay them $75,000.

1   I had insured the boat for $500,000. When I notified the insurance company that the
2   boat had sunk, I was told that the insurance company would not make a decision on the
3   claim until it determined what made the boat sink. The insurance company said that they
4   would send out a claims representative to be there while the boat was being worked on
5   and raised.
6
7   MRS began its work raising the boat on July 2, YR-2. They had two divers. The divers did
8   a survey of the boat, swimming around it and feeling to see if they could find any obvious
9   holes or gaps in the walls of the boat. They didn't find anything. They could tell that the
10   windows and doors had been knocked out. I have no idea how or why that was.
11
12   The plan was for the divers to use pieces of plywood to block up doors and windows to
13   make the boat water tight. I had sent them diagrams of the boat. I guess that should have
14   been my first hint as to their incompetence. I sent them the diagrams on my own; they
15   hadn't asked for them. And once they had the diagrams, they really didn't ask a lot of
16   questions about them.
17
18   Once the doors and windows were boarded up, MRS was to connect inflation bags to the
19   bottom of the boat, inflate them, and then float the boat up. While they never gave me a
20   definite time frame that it would take to do this, Keith certainly talked in terms of it just
21   taking a number of days. I got the definite understanding that this entire process would
22   not take more than two weeks.
23
24   The length of time that it would take to raise the boat was important to me. I was going
25   to be charged $1,000 a day to have Mobile Environmental Co. employees present, making
26   sure there weren't any environmental problems. My insurance didn't cover environmental
27   issues, so I was really concerned about diesel or hydraulic leaks during the recovery and
28   removal. Floating the boat up was the safest way to avoid those issues. And I was still
29   hoping that if the boat didn't stay underwater too long, I could repair it and save the boat.
30
31   Well, it turned out the people at MRS didn't know what they were doing. They put flotation
32   bags on the boat, but they put them on the surface of the water, not below the water line,
33   so they didn't do any good. They just floated like big beach balls. They pumped water out,
34   but the boat didn't come up at all. For some reason, water was still going in as fast as they
35   were pumping it out.
36
37   After a few weeks, Dolly Keith came to me and told me that the boat was too heavy and
38   that they needed to cut the boat. They needed to cut off the smokestacks, the railing, and
39   the floor of the top deck. According to Dolly, it was the only way that the boat could ever
40   be lifted. At that point, I still thought Dolly knew what she was doing, and I was still being
41   charged daily for the environmental standby, so I went along with it. It did mean, though,
42   that I probably wouldn't be able to save the boat. I knew that once she started cutting
43   the boat, odds were that it would not be repairable. She had me sign another agreement
44   giving her permission to cut the boat and sell any metal that they removed for salvage.
45   I didn't want to do it, but I didn't see that I had a choice.

1　MRS cut my boat. Dolly kept saying that they needed to make the boat lighter, that they
2　had to cut the steel floor to remove weight. They had to cut holes into the sides of the boat.
3　They had to purchase a special underwater torch and other specialized tools; I think that
4　they spent several thousand dollars on the equipment. Dolly never mentioned anything
5　to me about paying for that equipment until this lawsuit. I never saw any invoices.
6
7　Days turned into weeks and then months. When the summer had passed, I was really
8　concerned because the boat still hadn't moved. The relationship between Dolly and I was
9　very strained. She had told me when they started cutting the boat that I could no longer go
10　on the boat; all I could do was stand on the shore and watch them cut my boat up. It was
11　really painful and difficult. She wouldn't talk to me anymore; she would just walk by me.
12
13　After a while, it was becoming clear that Dolly was not going to be able to get the boat up.
14　I had talked to several people, including Rocky Roberts, one of the Mobile Environmental
15　Co. employees who had been on standby, and everybody was saying that MRS was over
16　its head; that they didn't have enough personnel, the proper equipment, or the expertise
17　to do the job. It should have been done in two or three weeks at the most. Every time that
18　I spoke with Keith, she told me that she had everything under control, that they were
19　making progress, and that cutting the boat was the best approach to be used.
20
21　In October, YR-2, I decided that I needed to do something. Enough was enough. I e-mailed
22　Dolly a letter telling her that this needed to come to an end and that we needed to talk.
23　I told her to stop everything until we could figure out how to get the boat up. Well, Dolly
24　just went off when she got that letter. She said that I had fired her. She packed up all of
25　her equipment and walked off of the job site. I wasn't firing her; I just wanted us to meet
26　and figure out a way to get the boat up. She never called me.
27
28　But, frankly, once I got over the shock of her leaving, I was kind of relieved she was gone.
29　That gave me the chance to hire Mobile Environmental Co. to get the boat up. It took them
30　just four days to pull the boat out, but then they used bulldozers and heavy equipment to
31　pull it. MRS didn't want to spend the money to rent the bulldozers. It cost me $65,000 for
32　Mobile Environmental Co. to pull the boat out and I still have an almost $100,000 bill for
33　the standby work that they did. MRS cost me that money.
34
35　Of course, as Mobile Environmental Co. pulled the boat out of the water, there was a lot
36　of stress on the boat. The seam that was created when I sealed the two halves of the boat
37　together pulled apart a little. Where the seam pulled apart looks like a hole.
38
39　On top of it, Dolly told Rocky Roberts and Murchison that I had fired her because I was
40　trying to hide the fact that I had deliberately sunk the boat. Dolly told that same nonsense
41　to Jerry Williams, my maintenance guy. I think that she talked to a bunch of people.
42
43　Dolly must have also told her lies to the insurance company. They denied my claim. In
44　the letter they sent me, they talked about some of the same things that Dolly wrote in her
45　letters to Murchison. Someone got Dolly's information to the insurance company. I'm in

1 a lawsuit with them right now to get my insurance payment. So far, I've been billed for
2 $25,000 in attorney's fees on that case and $10,000 in attorney's fees on this case.
3
4 And on top of it, Nita City terminated my lease. They invoked a clause in the lease that
5 required me to abide by all laws of the state and county. The termination letter said that
6 I attempted to defraud the insurance company. So because of Dolly, I lost the right to
7 control the dock where the Riverboat Queen had been docked for years. Even without
8 my boat, I would have been able to rent out the dock for at least $5,000 a month for the
9 fifteen months remaining on my lease.
10
11 All of this is so absurd. I built that boat with my own hands. My wife and I put a lot of
12 work into making it a business. It was our life's work. My wife, Elizabeth, had a terminal
13 illness. She was diagnosed in April YR-2 and her illness was quite costly. That's why the
14 boat sinking could not have come at a worse time. I didn't need those headaches when
15 I was trying to take care of my wife. She just died a couple of months ago.
16
17 Because Dolly didn't know how to run a business, she tried to destroy me and accused me
18 of deliberately sinking my boat. She needs to pay for all of the trouble she has caused me.
19
20
21 ## SUPPLEMENTAL STATEMENT:
22 ## GLENN V. INSUR-ALL INSURANCE COMPANY
23
24 The insurance company denied my claim. I have paid my premiums each and every
25 month on time. I was getting ready to renew my policy for another term when the boat
26 sank. I don't remember whether I received a letter from the insurance company telling
27 me that I had to have an inspection this time for them to insure the boat or not. Anyway,
28 it didn't make any difference because I was going to get the boat inspected. I was thinking
29 that I might need to increase my insurance coverage. I had contacted a boat inspector and
30 had arranged for the inspection. In fact, he was supposed to inspect the boat on June 15
31 so everything would be in place for the renewal. Unfortunately, that man's business card
32 was on the boat, and I don't remember his name. I hadn't done it earlier because running
33 the business by myself, taking my wife to all of her doctor's appointments, and taking
34 care of her had been pretty rough on me. I was juggling things the best that I could.
35
36 I called the insurance company the day the boat sank. After we got the boat up, it was
37 clear that it was a total loss. That's when I filed my insurance claim. I was shocked when
38 I received the letter denying my claim on the grounds that I had not properly maintained
39 the boat and that I had deliberately sunk my boat.
40
41 ## SUPPLEMENTAL STATEMENT: GLENN V. NITA CITY
42
43
44 When Nita City cancelled my lease, I couldn't believe it. All of the time that we were trying
45 to get the boat up, I was trying to develop alternate plans in case the Riverboat Queen

1 was totally destroyed. I had decided that I would buy a smaller boat with the insurance
2 money and run small private dinner cruises. I was beginning to see the boat sinking as
3 a blessing in disguise. I could captain the smaller boat by myself. It would be easier to
4 operate. That was important because with Elizabeth being sick she could no longer help
5 out. If my lease had not been terminated, I would have been able to operate another boat
6 and continue my business. If nothing else, I could have sub-let the dock.
7
8 ## SUPPLEMENTAL STATEMENT: STATE OF NITA v. FRED GLENN
9
10
11 I did not sink my boat. I built that boat with my own hands. I filed the insurance claim
12 because I believe that I am totally entitled to get paid for the loss of my boat. I had paid
13 my premiums. My boat sank, and I am entitled to that coverage.
14
15 The idea that I would do anything to risk dangerous fluids flowing into the lake is
16 ridiculous. The first place that I called when I learned the boat had sunk was the city to
17 make sure that someone had called an environmental company to put out booms. I made
18 certain that MRS did not cut holes into the deck anywhere near the hydraulic and diesel
19 tanks. I paid $1000 a day to have Mobile Environmental Co. out there every day that MRS
20 was working. I did everything that a responsible business owner should do.

DEPOSITION OF ROCKY ROBERTS

1   My name is Rocky Roberts. I work for Mobile Environmental Co. Mobile Environmental
2   Co. has several different business units. There is an environmental section, a construction
3   section, and a disaster relief section. I have worked in all of the sections, although I have
4   been most recently assigned to the disaster relief section. The environmental section
5   handles situations such as oil spills (pipelines, overturned tanker trucks, etc.), the
6   discharge of hazardous fluids and materials into bodies of water, and general disaster
7   relief. I've been involved in this type of business for almost twenty years since I graduated
8   from Nita University with a degree in environmental studies.

9

10   On June 14, YR-2, my company got a phone call from someone at Nita City reporting that
11   the Riverboat Queen had sunk. We were asked to immediately go to the lake and put
12   protection booms around the boat to keep any diesel or other fuels from seeping into the
13   water. This was important because the lake is a source of water for the city.

14

15   I was the head of the crew assigned to this project. I became responsible for setting the
16   booms and monitoring to see if there were any leaks. Booms are flotation devices that
17   float on the water and keep fluids from floating beyond them.

18

19   The City wanted someone from our company at the lake whenever anyone was on or
20   around the boat. For the first weeks, I kept a two-person crew at the boat every day, but
21   once the boat was settled into the bottom of the lake and it was clear no fuel was leaking
22   out, I pulled them off of the job.

23

24   I told Linda Murchison, the lady with the city, that I was pulling my crew off the job. She
25   got really angry and insisted that I bring them back. I told her that if she insisted, I'd bring
26   one person back, but that a two-person crew just wasn't necessary. The booms were
27   in place. Even if there was a leak, we could get out to the lake quickly and soak up any
28   leakage that might occur.

29

30   That first day, Mr. Glenn asked me if I knew of any companies that could possibly raise the
31   boat. I gave him Dolly Keith's telephone number. I had worked with her and her son a few
32   months earlier on another sunken boat. I told him that that boat had been a lot smaller,
33   though, and that I didn't know whether they had ever done any big boats. A few days later
34   Glenn told me that he had spoken with Dolly, that she seemed really nice, and that he was
35   going to use her company.

36

37   I was at the site the first day that MRS came on the job. I spoke with Dolly and Brad. They
38   were both eager to get started. Brad said that he had put together a plan to get the boat
39   up and that it shouldn't be too hard. He was going to close up all the windows and doors,
40   where water could flow into the boat, and then pump water out of the boat. Then they
41   were going to attach flotation bags, inflate them, and float the boat up. I've seen that
42   technique work lots of times; it's pretty basic in boat recovery.

1   MRS was on the job every day, even weekends, so either me or one of my guys had to
2   be out there. After a few days, MRS seemed to become frustrated. They couldn't get the
3   pumps to work right. They started blaming everybody for their problems. They especially
4   started talking bad about Mr. Glenn. They started saying that the way that the Riverboat
5   Queen was built, it was a surprise that it ever floated. Anytime Mr. Glenn would ask a
6   question, Dolly or Brad would get hostile, as if they resented him asking anything.
7
8   MRS had a guy, Rick Smart, who had the job of dive captain. He was supposed to be
9   in charge—he was the one who supervised the divers; ordered the equipment. He
10   supposedly had been in the Navy and he thought that he was something of an expert.
11
12   It was clear pretty early on, though, that the job was bigger than MRS had anticipated.
13   They only brought two divers when they really needed about five divers working together.
14   The divers used scuba tanks instead of umbilical cords (hoses attached to an air pump),
15   which allowed the divers to work more easily and for longer time periods.
16
17   The hoses that they used were too small to pump water out of the boat. They used two-
18   inch hoses when they should have had at least four-inch hoses for the pumps. Several
19   times I tried to talk with Smart about how the project was going, but he made it clear that
20   he didn't want to talk with me about it. Smart always acted as if he was indeed smarter
21   than me and that he didn't care what I thought.
22
23   In my opinion, at that point, even if MRS had just put the necessary manpower on the job,
24   it would not have been necessary to cut the boat up. If MRS had brought in enough divers,
25   they could have used other techniques that would have brought the boat up. But MRS was
26   trying to keep its expenses down and didn't bring on the necessary workers.
27
28   Then they started cutting the boat, and the situation just got worse. MRS really needed
29   more manpower. Brad and Rick were the only two cutting the boat, and that's a real
30   tedious process. You have to use a cutting torch and literally cut through the steel. They
31   took weeks to just cut off the top deck. In September and October I was talking with
32   Mr. Glenn, and I told him that I thought MRS was in over its head and that they had been
33   on the job too long not to have made more progress. I told him that at the rate that MRS
34   was going, the boat would not even be out of the lake by the end of the year. It was just
35   ridiculous what they were doing. I didn't know at the time that Mr. Glenn had agreed
36   that MRS could have the metal that they cut off. The price of metal sold as scrap would
37   certainly serve as an incentive for MRS to keep on cutting the boat up.
38
39   One day late in October, I came to the site and Dolly greeted me. She told me that I should
40   be happy, that Mr. Glenn had fired them, and that they were leaving the jobsite. She said
41   that she "was going to get every penny that Mr. Glenn owed them and then some." She
42   said that she "knew that Mr. Glenn had sunk that boat," that she "was going to make sure
43   that the necessary people knew that," and that he "would regret the day that he fired her."
44   She was really angry.

1 Brad was packing up their things. He was shaking his head a lot and kind of mumbling to
2 himself. He was saying things like "I didn't think this job would go this badly. I thought we could
3 handle it. I don't know what made it go wrong—was it Mr. Glenn? Or was it us?" You could tell
4 he was really upset. It was really strange; it was like he was having a conversation with himself.
5
6 I never saw the contract between Mr. Glenn and MRS. I know that it was taking too long
7 to get that boat up. There was no reason it should have taken that long. And I know that
8 Dolly and Brad were aware that someone from my company had to be there every day. In
9 fact, they had to call me and tell me when not to come. Surely they knew that my company
10 was being paid for me to be there.
11
12 After Dolly and Brad walked off the job, I saw Mr. Glenn. He showed me the letter that
13 he had sent to Ms. Keith. For the life of me, I don't understand how that letter could be
14 read as firing Ms. Keith. But, lucky for me, Mr. Glenn asked if I thought my company could
15 get the boat out. From having been out there each day, it was pretty clear to me that we
16 could hook some heavy chains to the boat and literally drag it out. It would take some big
17 bulldozers and earth moving equipment but I thought it could be done. I told Mr. Glenn
18 that and he hired us to get the boat out.
19
20 It took us about four days to get the boat out. We hired a couple of divers to inspect
21 the boat and get it ready to be dragged. They had to cut holes in the boat so that water
22 could drain from the boat as we pulled it out the water. We rented four bulldozers and a
23 backhoe. We attached two-inch metal cables from the bulldozers to the front of the boat.
24 The divers had cut holes on each side of bow and we ran the cable through that. The boat
25 pulled very slowly, but we were able to get it out of the lake. I think our bill was about
26 $65,000.00. I got a 5 percent commission for bringing the job to the company.
27
28 It really is a shame that MRS just didn't get the job done in the first place. Looking back,
29 I guess I thought that they had more experience than they did, and I overestimated their
30 abilities. And once they got in over their heads, they just wouldn't listen to anybody.
31
32 I've heard about Dolly's accusations that Mr. Glenn sank his own boat. That doesn't make
33 sense to me. Anyone who knows Mr. Glenn knows that he loved that boat like a member
34 of his family. He would never deliberately sink it. When we pulled the boat out we did find
35 a hole, but it wasn't very big. Nothing that would have caused the boat to sink. In fact, the
36 hole was probably formed when the boat was being pulled out. It's a mystery to me as to
37 what caused the boat to sink.
38
39
40
41
42
43
44
45

SUPPLEMENTAL STATEMENT:
GLENN V. INSUR-ALL INSURANCE COMPANY

43 I never met Bob Richardson, but I was there when he came out to the boat. He didn't bother
44 introducing himself to me. He walked right by me and went to talk to Dolly, Brad, and Rick.
45 I could hear him telling them that he was from the insurance company and that it was his job

1 to determine whether Mr. Glenn would get him insurance money or not. He told them that it
2 was really important for them to notice anything that didn't seem right and to tell him about
3 it. He said that if anything was suspicious, he wanted to know about it. That whole thing
4 seemed kind of strange to me. It sounded like he was actually asking them to spy on Mr. Glenn.
5
6
SUPPLEMENTAL STATEMENT: GLENN V. NITA CITY
7
8
9 Linda Murchison called my company and told us that the Riverboat Queen had sunk. She
10 asked that we come out and place booms around the boat to keep any of the boat fluids
11 from leaking into the lake. It was important to keep any fluids from entering the city's
12 water supply.
13
14 I had not met Linda before that phone call. I finally met her during one of her visits to the
15 site. She asked a lot of questions. She really wanted to know about everything that was
16 going on. She talked with Dolly Keith a lot. In fact, every time that she came to the lake,
17 she spent her time talking with Dolly; she really didn't have a lot to say to Mr. Glenn.
18
19 As I said, I don't know Linda, but I've heard that she really wasn't a very good real estate
20 person. The rumor on the street is that she got her job because she was from Nita and that
21 there was some family connection with someone in the office's property management
22 division, not because she knows anything or has experience in property management
23
24 I was shocked when I heard that she was under consideration for a promotion. But Linda
25 told Dolly that she was up for a pretty important promotion and getting the promotion
26 was going to depend on what happened with the Riverboat Queen. She told Dolly that she
27 needed to prove that she could make the hard decisions.
28
29
SUPPLEMENTAL STATEMENT: STATE OF NITA V. FRED GLENN
30
31
32 Mr. Glenn was really trying to bring the boat up so that he could get it repaired. While he
33 was waiting for MRS to raise the boat, we would talk about the repairs, wondering what
34 the damage would be, what it would take to get it fixed. Not once during all of those days
35 sitting with him waiting on MRS did he say anything that even raised any concerns or
36 questions about his sincerity.
37
38 I was the one who recommended MRS. I told him that I didn't know whether they had
39 ever raised any boats as big as the Riverboat Queen, but I certainly thought that they
40 could do it. This suggestion that Mr. Glenn deliberately hired a company that wouldn't be
41 able to raise the boat is ridiculous.
42
43 Glenn was always concerned about possible leakage into the lake. After all, we were there
44 to prevent any leakage and to blot up any spills that did occur. He certainly never would
45 do anything to risk a spillage.

DEPOSITION OF JEFFREY WILLIAMS

1   I love the water. Ever since I was a little kid I've loved being around boats. I'd worked
2   for Mr. Glenn for about four years before the boat sank. That was a special boat, the
3   Riverboat Queen. You didn't see many paddleboats in our part of the country—she was
4   quite a novelty.
5
6   Mr. Glenn was so proud of his boat. You could tell just how much work and attention he
7   devoted to the boat in terms of making sure all of the engines were working right and
8   keeping it looking good. All of the people who came to parties and weddings on the boat
9   were always real impressed.
10
11   We had a regular maintenance schedule for the boat. Every fifty trips we did a complete
12   engine check. Every spring I would go underwater and swim around the boat, checking
13   out the hull. There was never anything to suggest that there was a hole or an area where
14   there could be a hole.
15
16   I was on every trip that Mr. Glenn took with the boat. We never hit any objects or struck
17   any poles or anything that might cause damage to the boat. I don't know what made the
18   boat sink, but it wasn't anything that Mr. Glenn did.
19
20   The day that the boat sank, I got to the dock probably an hour after Mr. Glenn. You could
21   tell he was heartbroken. He was trying really hard not to break down crying, but you
22   could see the tears in his eyes. I saw him go talk with Rocky Roberts. When he finished
23   talking with Rocky, he came over to me and said that he had to find a company to bring
24   the boat up. He said that Rocky recommended a company, Marine Rescue and Salvage. He
25   said that it was a mother-and-son company.
26
27   Sometime later, Mr. Glenn told me that he reached a deal with Dolly Keith, the mother, to
28   get the boat out of the lake for $75,000. He told me that it was a flat fee contract with a no
29   cure, no pay clause. He explained that it meant that he would only have to pay $75,000 no
30   matter what expenses MRS incurred and that if they couldn't get the boat out of the lake,
31   he wouldn't have to pay them anything.
32
33   The morning that MRS started working was pretty hectic. In fact, the divers had brought
34   the equipment the night before. I helped them bring in some of the supplies. That morning,
35   they were actually in the water starting to inspect the boat before Dolly ever showed up.
36   I saw her give Mr. Glenn the contract. She said something, but I couldn't hear what she
37   said. I know that she helped Mr. Glenn sign the contract because she was holding it so that
38   he could use her palm for support as he signed it. It didn't take very long; I doubt that it
39   even took a full minute. It certainly wasn't long enough for him to have read it all.
40
41   Mr. Glenn really believed in Dolly, but I could see that she had sold him a bill of goods. She
42   didn't have nearly enough manpower to raise a boat that big. She was totally depending

1   on that guy, Rick Smart, to give the directions and figure out what needed to be done to
2   raise the boat. The problem was that they didn't have the right equipment or enough
3   people. I would often hear Smart complaining that he didn't have enough divers and that
4   he needed more divers to attach the flotation bags properly. You could tell that Smart was
5   just totally frustrated. A few times I saw him arguing with Dolly Keith. They would get
6   really animated arguing with each other, and they would raise their voices. I overheard
7   him telling Dolly, "You knew you weren't qualified to take on this job. You don't have the
8   equipment or the men. We can't do this." I couldn't hear what Dolly said in response, but
9   Smart actually stomped away like a little kid.
10
11 It was very difficult to watch Mr. Glenn every day. He was spending as much time as he
12 could at the boat, but his wife was very sick and he needed to be with her. The costs were
13 just mounting because he was paying for the environmental standby workers to be at the
14 dock every day.
15
16 One day Dolly suggested that they just cut the boat and remove some of the metal. She
17 said that the boat was too heavy to be raised off of the bottom of the lake. Because I know
18 Mr. Glenn so well, I knew that the idea of destroying the boat would kill him. But I think
19 by that time he just wanted it over, so he agreed.
20
21 I really thought that when they started removing parts of the boat that everything would
22 start moving along, but I was wrong. It got even worse. Only Rick and Brad Keith were
23 cutting. It took forever for them to use a torch to cut a 4-foot by 4-foot piece. With a boat
24 that was 110 feet long and 36 feet wide, it was going to take forever. But MRS was getting
25 the salvage. They were going to sell the metal that was being cut off of the boat. I don't
26 know how much they would get per pound, but a project like this they'd get $20,000
27 to $30,000 for the scrap metal—on top of their contract. They didn't have any labor
28 expenses with just the two of them cutting, so the salvage money was all theirs.
29
30 Mr. Glenn and I would talk about how long it was taking, how it shouldn't be taking so
31 long, and how much it was costing Mr. Glenn. We would talk about different things that
32 could be used to pull the boat out, such as bulldozers. Rocky Roberts made it quite clear
33 that he thought using bulldozers would work. In fact, some other boat people who came
34 around also suggested Mr. Glenn use bulldozers to just drag the boat out. They said he
35 needed to give up the idea of floating the boat up.
36
37 Well, things were getting worse with Mrs. Glenn, and I think Mr. Glenn just felt like he had
38 to do something. He wrote a letter to Dolly asking her to stop all work and to talk with her
39 about what could be done to get the boat up. He showed me the letter before he sent it to
40 Dolly. There was nothing in that letter that suggested he was firing her. I certainly didn't
41 think that the letter fired her.
42
43 Dolly sure stirred up a hornet's nest when she walked off the job. I heard her tell Linda
44 Murchison that she was sure that Mr. Glenn had deliberately sunk the boat to get the
45 insurance proceeds. She said that she knew that Mrs. Glenn was really sick and that the

1   medical bills were outrageous. She had overheard Mr. Glenn and me talking one day, when
2   he was telling me that he'd gotten another bill from the doctor. He was talking about how
3   he didn't know how he was going to pay all of the bills.
4
5
6   # SUPPLEMENTAL STATEMENT: STATEMENT: GLENN V. INSUR-ALL INSURANCE COMPANY
7
8
9   I don't know a lot about the details of the denial of Mr. Glenn's insurance claim. I do
10   know that it could not have come at a worse time for him. The medical bills were really
11   piling up. He hadn't been able to do any business for months because the boat sank, so
12   he didn't have any income. He was really counting on the insurance money to help him
13   pay off bills. This entire situation has not only caused Mr. Glenn a lot of problems, it has
14   really hurt his standing in the community. The boating community is a pretty small one,
15   especially when you have a boat the size of the Riverboat Queen. Mr. Glenn really was
16   viewed as very prominent and skilled—he built the boat himself. But when the rumors
17   started going around that Mr. Glenn sunk the boat intentionally, everyone's opinion of
18   him changed.
19
20
21   # SUPPLEMENTAL STATEMENT: GLENN V. NITA CITY
22
23   Losing the boat ramp lease cost Mr. Glenn more money. He had identified a boat that he
24   was going to purchase and set up on the ramp. He talked with me about that boat and
25   how it differed from the Riverboat Queen. We talked about it a lot when we were sitting
26   there watching the Keiths tear up the Riverboat Queen. He was definitely looking forward
27   to continuing doing business.
28
29
30   # SUPPLEMENTAL STATEMENT: STATE OF NITA V. FRED GLENN
31
32   I spent a lot of time around Mr. Glenn while we were watching them try to get the boat
33   up. He seemed genuinely concerned about the boat. He would talk a lot about when he
34   was building the boat and how much fun he had. He was really nostalgic. Based on my
35   observations, it is my opinion that there was no way that Mr. Glenn deliberately sank that
36   boat. There is also no way Mr. Glenn would ever do anything to risk fluids seeping into
37   the lake. Part of our regular maintenance included checking the fuel holding tanks. We
38   always made sure that they were sealed tight.

DEPOSITION OF STEVE PALMER

1 In the latter part of May, early June, YR-2, I got a phone call from Fred Glenn, the owner
2 of the Riverboat Queen. He told me that he had seen my ad in the Yellow Pages for boat
3 inspection. He told me that his insurance was coming up for renewal and that he needed
4 to arrange for an inspection of the boat.
5
6 I told Mr. Glenn that I had done a number of boat inspections for insurance companies.
7 I explained that I would need all of the records relating to the operations and maintenance
8 of the boat for the past year including records of all trips, number of hours that the
9 boat has cruised, oil changes, and hull inspections. Mr. Glenn said that producing the
10 documents would not be a problem and that he had them in the wheelhouse on the boat.
11
12 We made an appointment for me to go out to the boat a couple of days later. I went out to
13 the Riverboat Queen to meet with Mr. Glenn. I was going to get the records, review them,
14 and then do my actual inspection of the boat. But when I got out there, Mr. Glenn wasn't
15 there. His wife was in the hospital and something had come up that forced him to miss
16 our meeting. He called me to cancel the meeting, but I was already at the boat.
17
18 Anyway, since Mr. Glenn wasn't there, I really couldn't get any more detailed information
19 from him and I couldn't pick up the records. I did walk out the dock and onto the Riverboat
20 Queen. There was some guy there who worked for Mr. Glenn, but I don't remember his
21 name.
22
23 I didn't do an inspection of the boat. I just walked around. She seemed to be fairly solidly
24 built. It is really quite a unique boat; Mr. Glenn was quite ingenuous in his construction.
25 I doubt that anyone could duplicate it. He used a tractor engine to propel the paddles.
26 Fairly simple, but it works. The exterior of the boat, the part that I could see anyway, was
27 painted with and had no visible rust.
28
29 I didn't go into any of the crawl spaces and, needless to say, I never went underwater to
30 examine the exterior of the hull. Mr. Glenn was supposed to get back with me to actually
31 hire me to do the inspection, but I never heard from him again.

DEPOSITION OF BARBARA CAMPBELL

1   I retired from the Nita City Real Property Section in August, YR-2. I had worked for the
2   city for over thirty years. It had been a great place to work; everyone was committed to
3   serving the people of Nita. I started as a file clerk in the water department. After a few
4   years there, I was promoted to assistant administrative aide, working in the permits and
5   building department. That position involved working directly with the public, answering
6   questions and explaining our procedures and application processes. Then I got promoted
7   to administrative assistant in the same department.
8
9   About ten years before I retired, I transferred to the Real Property Section. That section
10 has, as one of its responsibilities, the oversight of Beacon Lake. It issues the permits for
11 businesses operating on the lake, oversees camping sites and special events, and manages
12 the dock leases.
13
14 I remember when Mr. Glenn brought the Riverboat Queen to the lake. It was such an
15 unusual boat and such a novelty attraction. We were quite excited. We thought that it
16 would bring tourists to Nita and expected it would bring in tourist revenue. The Riverboat
17 Queen became quite a landmark even though it never was the financial windfall that we
18 had anticipated.
19
20 In early YR-2, Linda Murchison became my direct supervisor. She is quite ambitious and
21 pushy. She openly tells people that she intends to be the city manager within the next
22 ten years. During one of our early meetings, she told me that she was focusing on making
23 all of the activities around the lake generate more revenue for the city. She was trying
24 to get the city manager to increase the costs for camping permits, fishing privileges,
25 and docks and leases. She was always talking about getting rid of Mr. Glenn and putting
26 another business in at that dock.
27
28 When the Riverboat Queen sank, Linda got very excited. I don't know who called her, but
29 when she hung up she came out of her office and said, "Barbara, this might be a golden
30 opportunity. Maybe we can finally get rid of Fred Glenn and that albatross boat of his and
31 put in a recreational boat and jet ski rental business that can really earn some money for
32 the city." She was actually very excited and energized.
33
34 I didn't go out to the lake while they were trying to get the Riverboat Queen up, but
35 Dolly Keith seemed to call Linda at the office just about every week. A couple of times
36 Linda mentioned that she was meeting with Dolly to find out what was going on with
37 the recovery efforts. After one of those meetings, Linda told me that she was convinced
38 that Mr. Glenn had sunk the boat to get the insurance proceeds. His insurance was about
39 to expire, and she had written him a letter reminding him that he had to have insurance
40 for his lease. She said the only way that the water could get into the boat was if there
41 was a hole in the boat somewhere. She said that Mr. Glenn was insisting that the boat be
42 dragged out of the lake, which would create holes in the boat. There would be no way to

1 tell if the holes were caused by dragging the boat or if they had existed previously. She
2 believed that dragging the boat out was Mr. Glenn's way of covering up what he had done.
3
4 While they were working to bring the boat up, Linda was getting frustrated. But she
5 believed that Dolly Keith was doing the best job possible. Besides, Dolly kept her up to date
6 on what was going on. But then Dolly called her and told her that Mr. Glenn had fired her.
7
8 That's when Linda really became convinced that Mr. Glenn was hiding something. She
9 told me that she would see that Mr. Glenn's lease was terminated, no matter what. She
10 was really upset when she said this.

DEPOSITION OF BOB RICHARDSON

1 I work as a claims adjuster for Insur-All Insurance Company. After high school, I joined
2 the Navy for two years. There really wasn't anything special about my time in the service
3 other than it confirmed just how much I love the water. I grew up in Connecticut, and we
4 were always boating on the New Haven Harbor and Long Island Sound.
5
6 After I got out of the Navy, I decided that I would go to college and get a degree in business.
7 I graduated from Nita University in YR-15. I was really lucky to get a job right out of
8 college with Insur-All. I actually started in the marketing department. Insur-All provides
9 customized insurance coverage for commercial entities, including commercial marine and
10 fleet automobile entities. One of our advertisements is, "Got a boat, give us a call. We insure
11 them all, big and small." We were real aggressive in our marketing campaigns. We had
12 fairly strict quota requirements for the number of policies each salesperson had to secure.
13
14 My first four years at the company, I worked in the commercial marine insurance sales
15 section selling policies to ferry boat owners, houseboat operators, commercial fishermen,
16 and charter boat owners. We have different types of coverage. Some policies insure the
17 boat itself, others include business operations.
18
19 Our policies often include conditions that have to be met before they become final.
20 We customarily issue a thirty-day binder, with the condition that the boat passes an
21 inspection. The inspection gives the insurance company the assurance that the boat meets
22 certain minimal marine standards. This is important because there are so many things
23 that can cause a boat to sink: the hull has not been properly maintained and started to
24 corrode, there are an insufficient number of bilge pumps to pump out water that might
25 get into the boat, or the boat does not have watertight compartments, such that water
26 entering one part of the boat flows into other areas. The inspection report also includes a
27 report about the maintenance and general condition of the boat. It is really important for
28 the insurance company to have that inspection report because the decision whether to
29 insure the boat, and at what premium cost, is dependent upon the condition of the boat.
30
31 It is the insured's responsibility to obtain an inspection by an approved marine inspector,
32 but a sales representative can waive that requirement. When that requirement is waived,
33 there is supposed to be a waiver form in the file.
34
35 The inspection report is particularly necessary when you're talking about a custom boat
36 like the Riverboat Queen. When a boat has been built by a nonprofessional it is even more
37 important to have a certified marine inspector check the seaworthiness of the boat. The
38 Riverboat Queen had seams where the front half and back half of the boat were joined.
39 The inspection report would have assessed the strength of the welds on those seams, the
40 amount of steel from each half that overlapped, and the thickness of the steel. All of that
41 information is important because a defect in any of them could cause the boat to sink.

1   We never got an inspection report on the Riverboat Queen. There isn't a waiver in the file,
2   so I don't know why there isn't an inspection report. Mr. Glenn should have provided such
3   a report. In fact, the thirty-day binder that we send out clearly states that the coverage
4   after the initial thirty days is dependent on a favorable inspection report. But we never
5   sent him a letter after the thirty-day period stating that the policy was rescinded.
6
7   The insurance coverage was due to expire on June 17, YR-2. We had sent Mr. Glenn a
8   letter dated May 17, YR-2, to tell him that the policy would not be renewed unless we
9   received an inspection report.
10
11   When Mr. Glenn called the company to report that the Riverboat Queen had sunk, the
12   claim was assigned to me. I spoke with him and wrote a memo about that telephone
13   conversation. Mr. Glenn seemed evasive and refused to answer some of my questions.
14   I repeatedly asked him when was the last time that the bottom of the boat had been
15   inspected and he kept saying he'd have to check. He couldn't even guess at a date. I asked
16   if it was last year or the year before, but he just kept saying he didn't know. I find that to
17   be very strange for a boat owner, particularly a commercial boat owner, because keeping
18   your boat well maintained is critical to running a boat business.
19
20   I decided that I would really look closely at this claim. When I pulled the file, of course the
21   first thing that I noticed was that the policy was due to expire in three days. Then I noted
22   that there wasn't an inspection report. There was even a letter in the file reminding Mr.
23   Glenn that he needed to send us that inspection report. I also noted that Mr. Glenn had
24   insured the boat for $500,000, but we didn't have anything to show that the boat was
25   worth that much. It was also interesting to me that Mr. Glenn didn't get the "business
26   operation" coverage or the "hull" or physical property coverage. Most commercial policies
27   also include the business operation because if something happens to the boat, they can't
28   run the business and they lose income.
29
30   I went out to the lake to see how the recovery process was going. I met Dolly and Brad
31   Keith. I had looked up their Web site before I went out to the lake. I noticed that they
32   did not seem to have any experience in raising a large boat. It was really strange that a
33   supposedly prudent businessman would use an inexperienced boat recovery company
34   to raise the boat.
35
36   When I was at the boat I also met Mr. Glenn. We only spoke briefly because he was so
37   distracted and preoccupied. At the time, I thought that perhaps he was overwhelmed by
38   seeing his boat underwater. I asked him to provide me with all of the records relating to
39   the boat. He never sent any records. I had told him that I needed those records to process
40   the claim, so it seemed very unusual to me that he did not produce them.
41
42   I was still concerned about the Keiths' experience. They planned to use flotation bags
43   to bring the boat up, which would allow us to inspect the boat and see what made it
44   sink. That was really my concern—why did the boat sink? Dolly Keith was certainly very
45   cooperative and helpful, answering all of my questions and volunteering information.

1   I spoke with her on a couple of occasions, getting updates from her. One time she called
2   me to tell me that Mr. Glenn was pushing her to use bulldozers to pull the boat out of the
3   lake. I really didn't want that to happen. Dragging the boat out would most likely make
4   it impossible for us to find out what caused the boat to sink. I had even told Glenn that
5   I wanted the boat floated up so I could have tests done to see what caused it to sink. If we
6   couldn't find out why it sank, we'd have to pay out the policy limits, namely $500,000.
7   I encouraged Dolly to keep on doing what she was doing and that floating the boat up was
8   the right way to go.
9
10 Then she called and told me that she had been fired. That's when I knew that Mr. Glenn
11 must have sunk the boat. Dolly and her crew had been doing everything that could be
12 done to get the boat up, and he fired her. It was clear to me that he was afraid that if the
13 boat came up, we'd see that he had done something to the boat. And then, in just a matter
14 of days, Glenn had arranged for the boat to be dragged out of the lake. Not surprisingly,
15 the boat came out of the water totally banged up. Where the two halves of the boat had
16 been welded together now had sections that had been pulled apart.
17
18 It was my decision that the insurance claim be denied.

DEPOSITION OF LINDA MURCHISON

1 I work for Nita City in their property management section. I oversee the boat dock where
2 the Riverboat Queen had been docked. I got this position in March YR-4. Before that,
3 I worked as a private real estate agent.
4
5 I first met Mr. Glenn when I started at the city. I visited with everybody who leased around
6 the lake. Mr. Glenn was a very pleasant man and was very eager to show me his boat. It
7 was clear that he was quite proud of his boat. He loved to tell the story of building the
8 boat, the first time it was launched, those kinds of things.
9
10 But I was concerned about his business volume. I mean, our rent isn't cheap, and I was
11 worried that he didn't have enough business. Over the years, Mr. Glenn has struggled to
12 make his rent payments. During the spring and summer he did okay with his cruises,
13 hosting proms, weddings, and parties. But during the fall and winter, he rarely had any
14 bookings. He seemed to struggle financially.
15
16 Then his wife got sick. Mr. Glenn didn't talk about her illness a lot. In fact, he didn't even
17 mention it until one day I asked about her. It was during one of my regular visits. I'd drop
18 by every few months. I just casually commented that I hadn't seen her in a while, and he
19 told me she had cancer. He said that it was difficult, but that she had really good doctors
20 and medical care. He was very optimistic about her treatment.
21
22 During the spring in YR-2, I noticed that the bookings of the Riverboat Queen were less
23 than they usually were. In fact, they were down about 50 percent. Under the lease, we get
24 monthly financial statements from our lessors. We want to be certain that the companies
25 leasing our properties are actually doing business.
26
27 I got a phone call from one of our officers with the Park Service on June 14, YR-2,
28 informing me that the boat had sunk. I immediately wondered what had happened. From
29 the paperwork that Mr. Glenn is required to provide us, I knew that his insurance would
30 expire on June 17, YR-2. We require all of the companies that provide services on our
31 property to have insurance, so that is something I closely monitor. In fact, I had sent Mr.
32 Glenn an e-mail on May 20, about a month before the insurance was to expire, inquiring as
33 to the status of his efforts to renew the insurance. I reminded him that his lease required
34 that he maintain insurance. I also reminded him that an inspection was needed. Mr. Glenn
35 never responded to that e-mail, so I sent him another e-mail on June 4. I stopped by the
36 ramp a couple of times after that to talk with him, but he was never there.
37
38 Given the decline in Mr. Glenn's business, Mrs. Glenn's medical bills, the upcoming
39 expiration of the boat's insurance, and the need for the inspection report at the time the
40 boat sank, I decided to try to get more information. I mean, it would not look good for
41 Nita City if one of our lessors was doing anything illegal. I wanted to be sure that the boat
42 was not intentionally sunk.

1   When Mr. Glenn hired Dolly Keith to raise the boat, I made it my business to stop by one
2   day to visit with her. I wanted to make certain that she was using the proper measures
3   and techniques to minimize any fuel leakage into the lake. The lake is a drinking water
4   source for the city, so spillage is a significant concern.
5
6   Dolly was quite pleasant, and we spent a little over an hour talking. She told me how
7   they were going to raise the boat, and introduced me to Rick Smart and her son. She
8   understood my concern about fuel leakage and confirmed that they would always have
9   someone with Mobile Environmental Co. at the site when they were working. She didn't
10   mention any problems with Mr. Glenn. Everything seemed fine.
11
12   I began to notice that Mr. Glenn started criticizing everything that Dolly did. He would
13   complain about where the holes were being cut to pump out the water. He wouldn't tell
14   them where all of the windows and doors were. He and Rocky Roberts would stand on
15   the shore line, just talking and pointing.
16
17   Then one day Dolly called me and told me that Mr. Glenn had sent her a letter informing
18   her that she was fired. She had my cell phone number. I asked her to e-mail me the letter.
19   She did, but I was out of the office for a week at a training course and didn't see the e-mail
20   until several days after it was sent. It was clear that Mr. Glenn told her to stop and not do
21   anymore work. In my book, that means she's fired. I was really upset at that point. I went
22   out to the lake to confront Mr. Glenn, but once again he wasn't around.
23
24   By the time that I actually was able to meet with Mr. Glenn, Rocky Roberts was already
25   using bulldozers to drag the Riverboat Queen out of the lake. I was furious. I had told
26   Rocky and Mr. Glenn that dragging the boat out would be too risky and could cause
27   significant fluid spillage into the lake. But it was clear that they both had ignored me.
28
29   Once the boat was onshore, it was clear that there had been deliberate damage to the
30   boat. The instant I learned that the insurance company had determined that it would not
31   pay the policy because it had concluded that Mr. Glenn had sunk the boat, I recommended
32   that the lease be terminated. I had already reached the same conclusion. I wrote a memo
33   to Scott Gardner, our city manager. It was Scott who signed the termination letter, but it
34   was based on my recommendation.
35
36   I feel sorry for Mr. Glenn, but that doesn't take away from the fact that I believe that he
37   had something to do with the boat sinking. A boat like the Riverboat Queen doesn't just
38   float one day and sink the next. There is always a reason.

Deposition of Scott Gardner

1   I am the city manager for Nita City. It is my duty and responsibility to make executive
2   decisions for the city. For most of the city contracts, I am actively involved in the
3   negotiation and development of the terms. We have city employees who are responsible
4   for overseeing and monitoring compliance with those contracts. Linda Murchison is
5   responsible for our real estate contracts and leases.
6
7   We have standard requirements for our commercial leases. Each business must have
8   commercial insurance with at least $400,000 in coverage in the event of any occurrence
9   on the premises. This is a necessary requirement to protect the city.
10
11 The requirement of insurance is especially important for boats like the Riverboat Queen.
12 We had specific provisions in Fred Glenn's lease that we don't include in other leases. For
13 example, he couldn't use glass or ceramic utensils because they could easily be broken.
14 The boat was supposed to be inspected at least every two years. Unfortunately, there isn't
15 any inspection report in the file. Apparently the employee who preceded Linda either
16 forgot to get the inspection or didn't file the report correctly.
17
18 The sinking of the Riverboat Queen was pretty big news in Nita. The Riverboat Queen
19 was a unique entertainment venue and was popular for school proms and special events.
20 I called Linda Murchison to make sure that she was aware of the boat sinking. I also told
21 her that I wanted her to stay on top of the situation because of possible environmental
22 issues that would be disastrous to the city. Linda was up for a promotion, and I told her
23 that how she handled this situation would be an important part of my assessment of her
24 performance for that promotion.
25
26 We have weekly staff meetings. After the boat sank and until it was dragged out of the
27 lake, Linda would give weekly reports about the efforts to get the boat out of the lake.
28 She seemed to have good handle on what was going on. She referenced conversations
29 with the crew that had been hired to raise the boat, the guy from the environmental
30 company, and even the insurance adjuster. She said that Mr. Glenn originally seemed very
31 insistent that he wanted to save the boat and get it repaired. Then all of a sudden he
32 changed his mind and just wanted the boat dragged out of the lake. This is just one of the
33 circumstances that troubled Linda.
34
35 After the boat was dragged out, Linda recommended that we terminate the lease. She
36 said that the evidence pointed to Mr. Glenn deliberately sinking the boat for the insurance
37 money. I had heard that Mrs. Glenn was very sick and that she needed a lot of medical
38 attention. Nita is pretty small, and the Glenns were well known. The medical bills had to
39 be very expensive.
40
41 Lisa told us that Mr. Glenn's business records showed a decline in business and that
42 Mr. Glenn wasn't making as much money as he used to. She also said that the insurance

1 policy was due to expire in just three more days. Mr. Glenn hadn't provided the inspection
2 report that was necessary to renew the policy.
3
4 Dolly Keith, the lady with the boat recovery company, told Linda that Mr. Glenn was
5 arguing with them about raising the boat. He was acting as if he had something to hide.
6 Floating the boat up would have allowed them to determine what caused the boat to sink.
7 By dragging it to the shore the way he did, Mr. Glenn made it impossible to find out what
8 caused the boat to sink.
9
10 All of these things gave us reason to believe that Mr. Glenn deliberately sank his boat to
11 get the insurance proceeds. Our lease is very favorable to the city. We're not a court of
12 law. We can terminate the lease if we have "reasonable basis" to believe that the lessor
13 has engaged in unlawful conduct. Based on all of the circumstances and factors, we had
14 a reasonable basis to believe that Mr. Glenn had violated the law, so we terminated his
15 lease.
16
17 Additionally, by sinking his boat, Glenn created a risk of toxic fuels spilling into the lake.
18 He had both diesel and hydraulic fluids on his boat. When a boat goes down, you can
19 never be sure that the fluids will not leak into the water.

CIRCUIT COURT OF DARROW COUNTY
STATE OF NITA

MARINE RESCUE AND SALVAGE   )

      (MRS)   )

)

v.   )   CAUSE NO: 2012-328

)

FRED GLENN, dba RIVERBOAT QUEEN   )

)

COMPLAINT

COMES NOW, the Plaintiff, MARINE RESCUE AND SALVAGE (MRS), and for cause of action against the Defendant FRED GLEN, dba RIVERBOAT QUEEN alleges:

1) At all times relevant to this case, the Plaintiff was a partnership duly authorized to conduct business in the State of Nita.

2) At all times relevant to this case, the Defendant was the owner and operator of an entertainment riverboat named the Riverboat Queen.

3) On or about June 14, YR-2, the Riverboat Queen sank in Beacon Lake.

4) Fred Glenn contacted MRS to raise the boat and to remove it from the lake.

5) MRS contracted with Fred Glenn to raise the boat and to remove it from the lake.

6) A written contract was entered that required Glenn, among other things, to pay MRS $75,000 to raise the boat and to remove it from the lake.

7) Under the contract, Glenn was also to reimburse MRS for additional expenses incurred in raising the boat.

8) Glenn, after entering into the contract with MRS, embarked upon a course of conduct that interfered with MRS' ability to perform under the contract.

9) Glenn's actions made it impossible for MRS to meet its obligations under the contract.

10) Glenn, without reason or justification, terminated the contract when he directed MRS to cease all activity to raise the Riverboat Queen from the lake.

11) The Defendant refuses to pay MRS the $75,000 to which it would have been entitled if Glenn had not breached the contract.

12) The Defendant refuses to pay MRS the sum of $17,500, which was incurred for the rental of special equipment that was used in the work to raise the Riverboat Queen.

13) Because of the Defendant's breach of the contract, the Plaintiff was forced to cease doing business.

RELIEF SOUGHT

WHEREFORE, it is respectfully requested that judgment be entered against the Defendant and that the Plaintiff be awarded damages in the amount for $500,000 actual and special damages that were sustained as a result of the Defendant's wrongful actions and any other such relief to which the Plaintiff may be entitled.

JURY DEMAND

Plaintiff demands a jury trial in this action.

Franklin Gibson

FRANKLIN GIBSON
Attorney for Plaintiff
508 Elm Street
Nita City, Nita 88888
(555) 532-9876

CIRCUIT COURT OF DARROW COUNTY
STATE OF NITA

MARINE RESCUE AND SALVAGE)
          (MRS))
)
)
v.) CAUSE NO: **2012-328**
)
)
FRED GLENN, dba RIVERBOAT QUEEN)

ANSWER AND COUNTERCLAIM OF FRED GLENN dba RIVERBOAT QUEEN

COMES NOW, the Defendant, Fred Glenn dba Riverboat Queen, and in answer to the Plaintiff's Complaint states:

I.

1) The Plaintiff fails to state a claim upon which relief can be granted.

II.

2) The Defendant admits the allegations set forth in Paragraphs 2, 3, and 4.

3) The Defendant denies the allegations set forth in Paragraphs 5, 6, 7, 8, 9, 10, 11, 12, and 13.

4) The Defendant denies that the Plaintiff is entitled to any relief that is sought.

FIRST AFFIRMATIVE DEFENSE

1) Marine Rescue and Salvage (MRS), Dolly Keith, and Brad Keith failed to raise and remove the Riverboat Queen and under the "no cure, no pay" provision is not entitled to any compensation.

SECOND AFFIRMATIVE DEFENSE

1) Marine Rescue and Salvage (MRS), Dolly Keith, and Brad Keith abandoned their efforts to raise and remove the Riverboat Queen.

WHEREFORE, the Defendant demands that the complaint be dismissed and judgment entered in favor of the Defendant with costs and such other and further relief as the Court may deem appropriate.

COUNTERCLAIM

COMES NOW the Counter-Plaintiff, Fred Glenn dba Riverboat Queen, and for cause of action against the Counter-Defendant Marine Rescue and Salvage alleges:

1) At all times relevant, MRS, Dolly Keith, and Brad Keith held themselves out as experts in boat and marine recovery.

2) Marine Rescue and Salvage (MRS), Dolly Keith, and Brad Keith misrepresented their qualifications and experience to raise and remove a boat the size of the Riverboat Queen.

3) Based on the false, fraudulent, and misleading representations of Dolly Keith, Brad Keith, and other representatives of MRS, Glenn was induced to enter into a contract with Marine Rescue and Salvage.

4) Marine Rescue and Salvage (MRS), Dolly Keith, and Brad Keith did not have the experience, qualifications, and equipment necessary to raise the Riverboat Queen.

5) As a consequence of the misrepresentations and fraudulent conduct of MRS, Dolly Keith, and Brad Keith, the Riverboat Queen was completely destroyed.

6) As a consequence of the misrepresentations and malicious actions of MRS, Dolly Keith, and Brad Keith, Glenn's lease with Nita City was terminated.

7) As a consequence of the misrepresentations of MRS, Dolly Keith, and Brad Keith, Glenn was required to secure the services of Mobile Environmental Co. on a daily basis to protect against any adverse environmental consequences.

RELIEF SOUGHT

WHEREFORE, it is respectfully requested that judgment be entered against the Counter-Defendant and that the Counter Plaintiff be awarded damages in the amount of $500,000 for actual and consequential damages that were sustained as a result of the Counter- Defendant's wrongful actions.

Cecilia Mann

CECILIA MANN
Attorney for Defendant/Counter-Plaintiff
286 Bethany Street
Nita City, Nita
(555) 532-9876

CIRCUIT COURT OF DARROW COUNTY
STATE OF NITA

FRED GLENN, dba RIVERBOAT QUEEN	)	
	)	
	)	
v.	)	CAUSE NO: **2012-543**
	)	
	)	JURY TRIAL DEMANDED
INSUR-ALL INSURANCE COMPANY	)	

COMPLAINT

COMES NOW the Plaintiff, FRED GLENN DBA RIVERBOAT QUEEN, and for cause of action against the INSUR-ALL INSURANCE COMPANY alleges:

1) At all times relevant to this case, the Plaintiff was a resident of Darrow County, Nita.

2) At all times relevant to this case, Insur-All Insurance Company was a company licensed to issue insurance policies in the state of Nita.

3) Fred Glenn was the owner and operator of a riverboat called the Riverboat Queen.

4) Glenn purchased insurance coverage in the amount of $500,000 from Insur-All Insurance Company. A true and correct copy of the insurance policy is attached to this Complaint.

5) At all times relevant to this case, Glenn timely paid all insurance premiums and satisfied all conditions precedent required by the policy.

6) On or about June 14, YR-2, the Riverboat Queen sank on Beacon Lake in Nita City, Darrow County.

7) On or about November 14, YR-2, Glenn filed a claim with Insur-All Insurance Company for payment due to the sinking and complete destruction of the Riverboat Queen.

8) Insur-All Insurance Company refuses to pay the Plaintiff the sum of $500,000 as required by the terms of the insurance policy.

FIRST CLAIM FOR RELIEF—BREACH OF CONTRACT

The Plaintiff is entitled to damages in the amount of $500,000 for breach of contract by Insur-All Insurance Company in its failure to pay to the Plaintiff, upon proper demand, the amount of the insurance policy coverage.

SECOND CLAIM FOR RELIEF—BAD FAITH

Insur-All Insurance Company acted in bad faith when it refused to pay the Plaintiff the proceeds of the insurance policy upon submission of the claim. The Plaintiff is entitled to damages triple the amount of the face value of the policy, amounting to $1,500,000.

WHEREFORE, the Plaintiff demands judgment against the Defendant for compensatory and punitive damages.

Cecilia Mann

CECILIA MANN
Attorney for Plaintiff
286 Bethany Street
Nita City, Nita
(555) 532-9876

CIRCUIT COURT OF DARROW COUNTY
STATE OF NITA

FRED GLENN, dba RIVERBOAT QUEEN   )

)

)

v.   )   CAUSE NO: **2012-543**

)

INSUR-ALL INSURANCE COMPANY   )

ANSWER

COMES NOW, INSUR-ALL INSURANCE COMPANY, the Defendant and in answer to the Plaintiff's Complaint states:

I.

1) The Plaintiff fails to state a claim upon which relief can be granted.

II.

2) The Defendant admits the allegations in paragraphs 1–8.

3) The Plaintiff failed to meet all conditions precedent to the payment of any proceeds in that the Defendant failed to submit an inspection report setting forth the condition of the vessel.

FIRST AFFIRMATIVE DEFENSE

4) The Plaintiff breached the terms of the insurance company when he failed to properly maintain the vessel.

SECOND AFFIRMATIVE DEFENSE

5) Because the sinking of the Riverboat Queen was not the result of ordinary wear of a marine vessel, but was caused by a breach in the hull, there is no coverage under the insurance policy.

THIRD AFFIRMATIVE DEFENSE

WHEREFORE, the Defendant demands that the complaint be dismissed and judgment entered in favor of the Defendant with costs and such other and further relief as the Court may deem appropriate.

Bailey Brown

Bailey Brown
Attorney for Defendant
1033 Jackson Road
Nita City, Nita
(555) 435-2903

CIRCUIT COURT OF DARROW COUNTY
STATE OF NITA

FRED GLENN, dba RIVERBOAT QUEEN)

)

)

v.) CAUSE NO: **2012-544**

)

) JURY TRIAL DEMANDED

NITA CITY)

COMPLAINT

COMES NOW, the Plaintiff, FRED GLENN DBA RIVERBOAT QUEEN, and for cause of action against NITA CITY alleges:

1)   At all times relevant to this case, the Plaintiff was a resident of Darrow County, Nita.

2)   Nita City is a municipal organization formed under the laws of the state of Nita and is amenable to suit because the cause of action arises from Nita City's ownership and leasing of real estate, which is not a governmental action protected by sovereign immunity.

3)   The Plaintiff owned an entertainment riverboat, The Riverboat Queen.

4)   Beginning in January YR-3, the Plaintiff leased a commercial dock from the Defendant. At all times material hereto, the Plaintiff has paid, on time, all rental costs that were due under the lease.

5)   Pursuant to the lease terms, the Plaintiff renewed the lease for a second five-year term on February 2, YR-2.

6)   On June 14, YR-2, the Riverboat Queen mysteriously sank.

7)   The Plaintiff notified Linda Murchison, Property Manager for Nita City.

8)   Linda Murchison advised the Plaintiff that she had already been informed that the Riverboat Queen had sunk and had contracted for Mobile Environmental Co. to provide protective environmental services to prevent the leakage of dangerous fluids into Beacon Lake.

9)   Pursuant to Linda Murchison's instructions, the Plaintiff generally kept Murchison apprised of the efforts to raise and remove the Riverboat Queen.

10) Upon information and belief, Murchison approached Dolly Keith, one of the owners of Marine Rescue and Salvage, who had been hired to raise the Riverboat Queen.

11) Upon information and belief, Murchison and Dolly Keith communicated regularly.

12) Upon information and belief, Dolly Keith told Murchison that the Plaintiff was responsible for the sinking of the Riverboat Queen.

13) Based upon the information received from Dolly Keith, Murchison wrote a letter terminating the lease between Nita City and the Plaintiff.

14) As a result of the termination of the Plaintiff's lease, the Plaintiff was not able to dock an alternate boat at the boat ramp and continue his business.

15) Nita City did not have a valid reason for the termination of the lease.

16) Nita City breached its contract with the Plaintiff, causing the Plaintiff damages.

17) The Plaintiff is entitled to damages in the amount of $500,000 for the breach of contract by Nita City in its wrongful termination of the lease.

WHEREFORE, the Plaintiff demands judgment against the defendant, Nita City, for compensatory damages.

Cecilia Mann

Celia Mann
Attorney for Plaintiff
286 Bethany Street
Nita City, Nita
(555) 532-9876

CIRCUIT COURT OF DARROW COUNTY
STATE OF NITA

FRED GLENN, dba RIVERBOAT QUEEN)
)
)
v.   ) CAUSE NO: **2012-544**
)
NITA CITY   )

ANSWER

COMES NOW, NITA CITY, the Defendant and in answer to the Plaintiff's Complaint states:

I.

1) The Plaintiff fails to state a claim upon which relief can be granted.

FIRST AFFIRMATIVE DEFENSE

The Defendant breached the conditions of the lease agreement by engaging in conduct that gave Nita City reason to believe that he was violating Nita Criminal Statutes.

WHEREFORE, the Defendant demands that the complaint be dismissed and judgment entered in favor of the Defendant with costs and such other and further relief as the Court may deem appropriate.

Tyler Johnson

Tyler Johnson
Assistant City Attorney
Nita City Hall
529 Washington Streets
Nita City, Nita
(555) 761-3592

CIRCUIT COURT OF DARROW COUNTY
STATE OF NITA

STATE OF NITA	)	
	)	
v.	)	CAUSE NO: **2012-583**
	)	
FRED GLEN	)	

INDICTMENT

The Grand Jury charges:

COUNT 1

On or about June 14, YR-2, Defendant FRED GLENN, as the owner and operator of the Riverboat Queen, did knowingly or recklessly cause a condition that led, or could lead to, the discharge of pollutants into a water of the state, to wit, Beacon Lake, when he knowingly or recklessly caused the sinking of the Riverboat Queen, an entertainment paddleboat.

In violation of Nita Water Hazards Act (Pollution)

COUNT 2

On or about November 14, YR-2, Defendant FRED GLENN, as the owner and operator of the Riverboat Queen, did submit a false and fraudulent claim for insurance proceeds to Insur-All Insurance Company knowing that at the time of said claim for insurance proceeds that he was not lawfully entitled to any such payment.

In violation of Nita Criminal Statutes, Sections 42.5 (Insurance fraud)

A True Bill.

Richard Thompson

Richard Thompson
Foreman of the Grand Jury

Exhibit 1

Riverboat Queen—One year before it sank, side view

Exhibit 2

Riverboat Queen—One year before it sank, rear view

Exhibit 3

Riverboat Queen—Stairwell to upper deck and wheelhouse

Exhibit 4

Interior of lower deck

Exhibit 5

Riverboat Queen—Diagram of lower deck

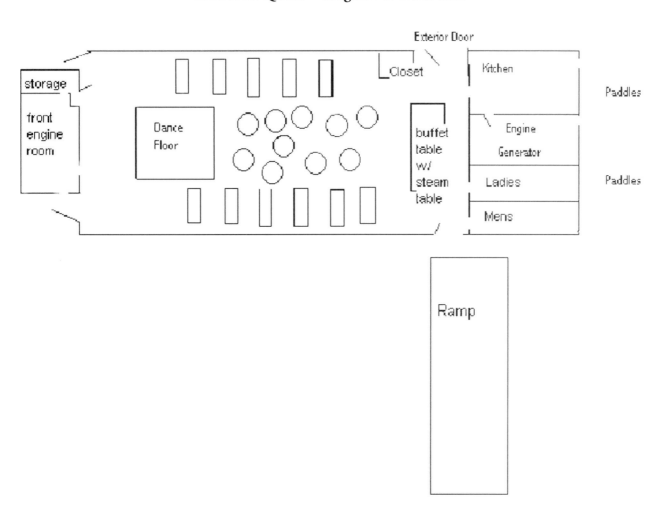

Exhibit 6

Riverboat Queen—Diagram of lower deck front engine room

**FRONT
ENGINE ROOM**

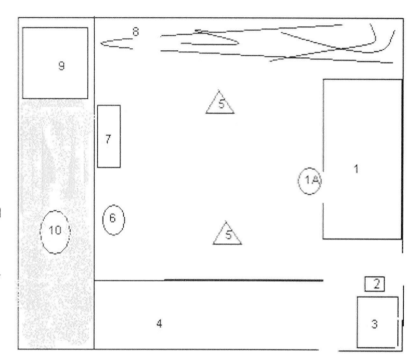

1/1A: Diesel engine with muffler piped under floor plating
2: Thruster pump - underneath - faucet extends through floor
3. Furnace
4. Sloped ceiling storage area; electric boxes on both sides of wall
5. Gear boxes w/ chains -- underneath, operate the thrusters/ propellers
6: Air tank, underneath ledge/shelf
7: 3 bilge/septic pumps, underneath ledge/shelf
8: Hoses for hydraulic system
9. Hydraulic storage tank
10. Portable air compressor

Exhibit 7

Riverboat Queen—Diagram of kitchen

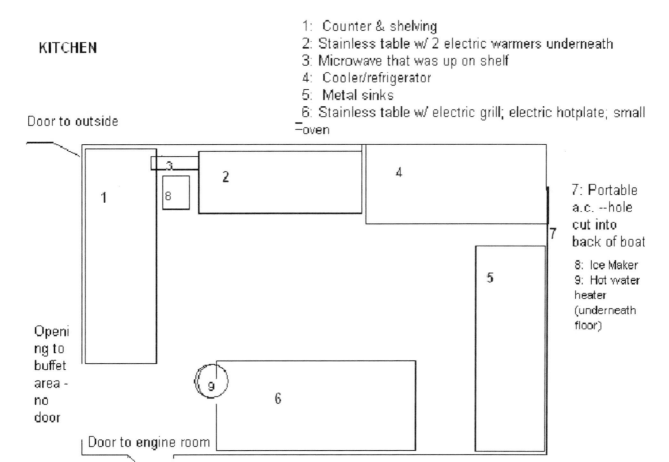

KITCHEN

1: Counter & shelving
2: Stainless table w/ 2 electric warmers underneath
3: Microwave that was up on shelf
4: Cooler/refrigerator
5: Metal sinks
6: Stainless table w/ electric grill; electric hotplate; small oven

Door to outside

7: Portable a.c. --hole cut into back of boat

8: Ice Maker
9: Hot water heater (underneath floor)

Opening to buffet area - no door

Door to engine room

Exhibit 8

Riverboat Queen—Diagram of rear engine room (lower level)

REAR ENGINE ROOM -- accessed through kitchen

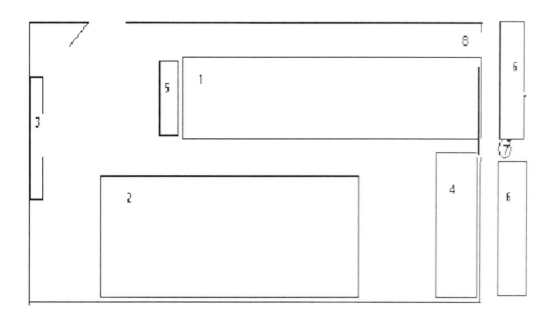

NOT DRAWN TO SCALE

1: Diesel engine bolted to floor
2: Generator raised on blocks
3: Electrical panels/breaker boxes; portable AC unit; shelves
4: Recessed septic holding area
5: Shelves/mop sink
6: Paddles
7: Propeller shaft
8: Gate to back of boat; outside

Exhibit 9

Riverboat Queen—Diagram of upper deck

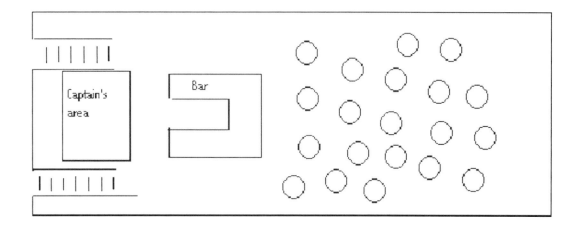

Exhibit 10

Riverboat Queen—Diagram of hull

HULL DIAGRAM

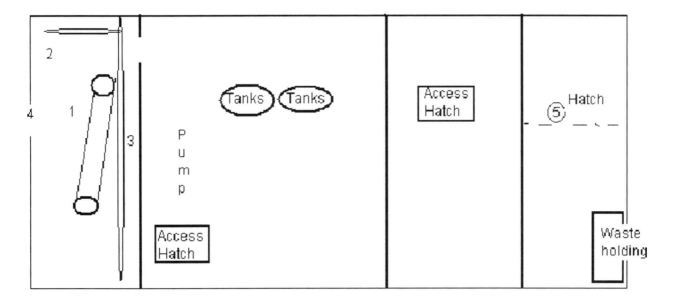

1: Gears with chains
2: Pipes
3: Muffler pipes
4: Septic holding tank

5. Hot water heater

Exhibit 11

Riverboat Queen—Day it sank (environmental booms have been placed around the boat)

Exhibit 12

Ex. 12: Riverboat Queen—Day it sank, close-up view

Exhibit 13

Rear of Riverboat Queen—Paddles sticking up out of water; diesel floating on water

Exhibit 14

Brad Keith in his scuba gear

Exhibit 15

Top deck, before cutting by MRS

Exhibit 16

Hole cut into the floor of top deck

Exhibit 17

Water being pumped out of the lower deck

Exhibit 18

Flotation bags floating on top of the water

Exhibit 19

Water being pumped out of the front engine room

Exhibit 20

Riverboat Queen—Blue line showing initial water level

Exhibit 21

Top deck with canopy being removed and stacked

Exhibit 22

Canopy posts being stacked for salvage

Exhibit 23

Side view with canopy removed

Exhibit 24

Top decking being removed

Exhibit 25

Top decking being removed

Exhibit 26

Top decking almost totally removed

Exhibit 27

Equipment used to pull the boat out of the lake

Exhibit 28

Additional Equipment Used to Pull the Riverboat Queen out of the lake

Exhibit 29

Riverboat Queen being dragged to shoreline

Exhibit 30

Riverboat Queen being dragged to shoreline

Exhibit 31

Metal cut off of the boat

Exhibit 32

More metal cut off of boat

Exhibit 33

One piece of Riverboat Queen hull with a hole

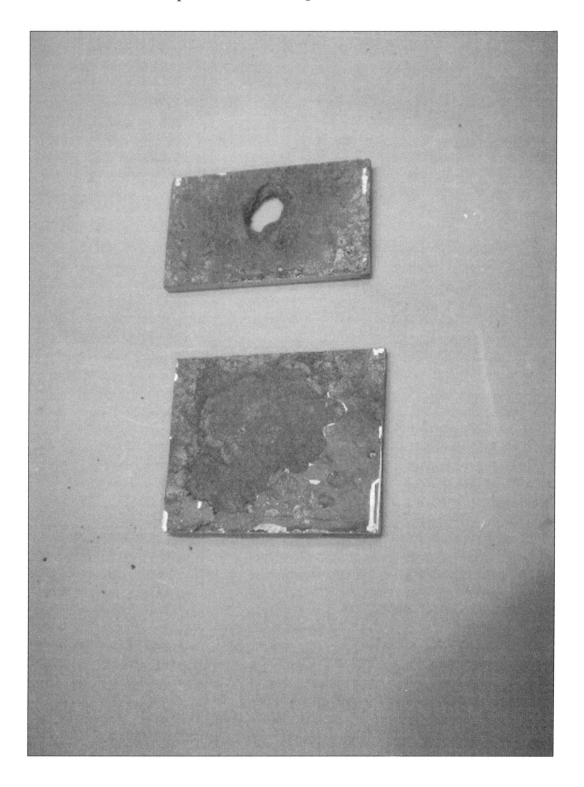

Exhibit 34

Second piece of Riverboat Queen hull with a hole (with a ruler)

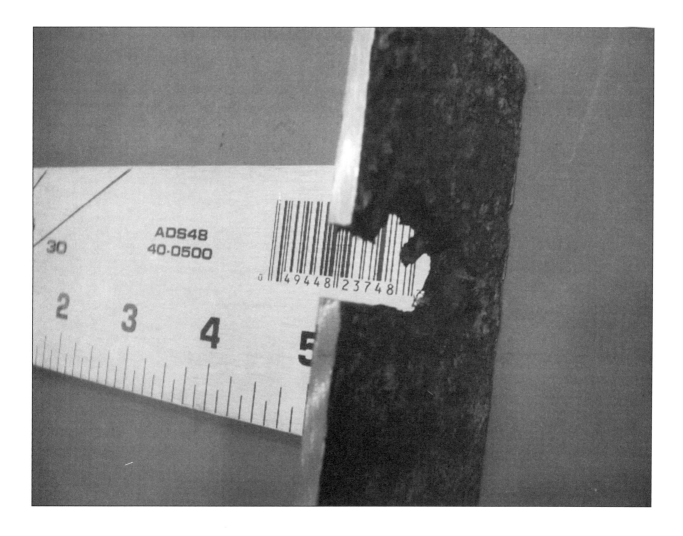

Exhibit 35

BOAT RECOVERY CONTRACT

Parties:

Marine Rescue and Salvage (MRS) is a boat Recovery and Salvage Company.
Fred Glenn owns and operates The Riverboat Queen, a 115-foot paddleboat that sank in Beacon Lake in Nita City.   **FG**

Services:

MRS contracts with Fred Glenn to provide Recovery and Salvage services with respect to the Riverboat Queen. The Riverboat Queen sank on June 14, YR-2 and has been partially submerged since that date.   **FG**

MRS will provide divers, equipment, materials, and procedures necessary to raise the Riverboat Queen and remove the vessel from the lake. MRS will pump the water out of the vessel and use flotation devices to raise the boat.   **FG**

MRS will utilize sling straps for attachment of the flotation devices.   **FG**

If extra manpower, extra equipment, or equipment not routinely used in the Recovery and Salvage of boats is needed, the cost of either the rental or purchase of said equipment will be billed to Fred Glenn.   ——

Special Provisions:

"No Cure – No Pay" Clause: Should MRS be unable to recover and salvage the Riverboat Queen, MRS will not be entitled to any payment or compensation for the work that it performed.   **FG**

"Promise of Co-operation" Clause: Because MRS must rely upon information provided by Glenn to provide services, Glenn promises to co-operate fully with MRS; in the failure to provide such co-operation, Glenn is responsible for paymentof the entire contracted amount and any and all damages that may flow from that lack of cooperation.   **FG**

Exclusions:

MRS assumes no responsibility for any damage(s) to the vessel during
the Recovery and Salvage process. MRS assumes no responsibility for
any fuel or liquid seepage into the water, or the pollution of any water
supply or damage to wildlife, property, or land.   **FG**

Payment:

Fred Glenn shall pay the base sum of $75,000 to MRS for its services
and work in the Recovery and Salvage of the Riverboat Queen.   **FG**

Dolly Keith   *Fred Glenn*

on behalf of Marine Rescue and Salvage

Exhibit 36

From: MRS, marinerescue@nita.com
Sent: June 28, YR-2, 3:45 pm
To: Riverboat Queen, riverboat@nita.com

We'll get started on July 2nd. I'll bring the contract with me, and you can sign it at that time. Then I'll make you a copy of the signed document and get it to you. I know that this has been a terrible situation for you. Rest assured that MRS and our team will do our best to get the boat up and help you find out why she sank.

Exhibit 37

From: Riverboat Queen, riverboat@nita.com
Sent: June 28, YR-2, 1:30 pm
To: MRS, marinerescue@nita.com

Thanks for the bid. Let's do it. Get the boat up for $75,000. I need to know why the boat sank so I can see if I can fix her and get her up and cruising again. We can't tell that until we get her up.

Exhibit 38

From: MRS, marinerescue@nita.com
Sent: June 25, YR-2 11:00 am
To: Riverboat Queen, riverboat@nita.com

Fred,

On behalf of Marine Rescue and Salvage, I am pleased to send you a bid for raising the Riverboat Queen. Based upon the information available, and subject to the same, MRS will raise the Riverboat Queen for the fee of $75,000.00, assuming customary and ordinary expenses. Your boat is obviously bigger than the average pleasure boat, but the same principles that raise small boats will raise large boats—buoyancy will raise heavy objects. It shouldn't take too long to get it up, and then you can decide what to do with it.

Let me know if you're interested in this bid and I'll send you a contract.

Dolly

Exhibit 39

From: MRS, marinerescue@nita.com
Sent: June 15, YR-2, 10:30 am
To: Riverboat Queen, riverboat@nita.com

Hi Fred. Got your e-mail. Recovering boats is certainly what we do. I'll send a couple of my guys out to check out the situation and get back with you about a bid. The way that I do business is this: I charge a fee to get the boat raised using flotation bags and sling straps and pumping the water out. There's always a slight possibility that that approach won't work, and we'll have to take a different approach. But we don't give up and we've always gotten the boats up. We'll stay on a job as long as it takes. But if I can't get the boat out, you don't have to pay me anything. In the recovery industry, such a "no cure, no pay" provision is fairly standard.

I'll send you a bid once we've had a chance to look at the boat. In the meantime, hang in there. I know that it must be rough because the Riverboat Queen was not just your boat, it was your livelihood.

Exhibit 40

From: Riverboat Queen, riverboat@nita.com
Sent: June 14, YR-2 4:15 pm
To: MRS, marinerescue@nita.com

As I told you during our telephone conversation, my boat has sunk. It is a double decker paddleboat, approximately 115 feet long, 36 feet wide. It was big enough to hold 350 passengers. We operated as dinner cruise boat. We also did private parties and special events.

I need to get the boat raised and determine what caused it to sink. Depending upon the damage, I may get the boat repaired. We'll just have to see about that.

I need to get an estimate on getting the boat raised. From our conversation, you seem to be up to the job. Can you get me an estimate?

Exhibit 41

From: Riverboat Queen, riverboat@nita.com
Sent: October (DATE)
To: MRS, marinerescue@nita.com

Ms. Dolly Keith
Marine Rescue and Salvage

October 25, YR-2

Dear Dolly,

I am very concerned about how long this job has been taking. You and your people seem to have been working diligently on the boat, but it seems like very little has been achieved. It does not appear that the boat is significantly closer to be raised off of the bottom of the lake than it was when you started.

You know that I cannot afford for you to keep going on the way you are. Each day that you are out there is costing me $1,000 for Mobile Environmental Co. to be standby.

Please don't come out to the lake anymore until we can figure out something else that can be done. It's obvious that your approach is not working, and I need an approach that will work. Things have to change.

I look forward to hearing from you.

Fred

Exhibit 42

INSUR-ALL INSURANCE COMPANY
POLICY OF INSURANCE #890-938

Insur-all insurance company, hereinafter referred to as "The Company," IN CONSIDERATION of the application for this Policy, and in further consideration of the premiums hereinafter stated does hereby insure THE RIVERBOAT QUEEN, a paddleboat owned by Fred Glenn.

FACE AMOUNT OF THE POLICY: $500,000.00
BENEFICIARY: Fred Glenn
ANNUAL PREMIUM: $2,500.00

OPERATION OF VESSEL: Owner warrants and expressly represents that the vessel will only be used for entertainment and restaurant purposes, such purpose and use being a condition of this policy.

MAINTENANCE OF VESSEL: Owner warrants and expressly represents that the vessel will be properly maintained in accordance with marine standards, such maintenance being a condition of this policy.

Upon demand of The Company, the owner shall provide to The Company an inspection report that details the condition of the vessel, such provision of an inspection report being a condition of this policy.

The Company reserves the right to cancel this policy and deny coverage for any claimed incident if the vessel is not used in accordance with the stated purpose or is not maintained in accordance with marine standards.

IN WITNESS WHEREOF, THE INSUR-ALL INSURANCE COMPANY has caused this Policy to be executed and duly attested at its office in Nita City, Nita on the 17th day of June, YR-3.

Margaret Hudson

Margaret Hudson

Peter Wilson

Peter Wilson

A copy of this policy has been mailed to:

Mr. Fred Glenn
The Riverboat Queen
P.O. Box 123
Nita City, Nita 88888

Exhibit 43

INSUR-ALL INSURANCE COMPANY
338 MAIN STREET
NITA CITY, NITA 88890

May 17, YR-2

Mr. Fred Glenn
The Riverboat Queen
P.O. Box 123
Nita City, Nita 88888

 Re: *Policy #* 890-938

Dear Mr. Glenn:

This letter is to remind you that your policy will be expiring on June 17, YR-2. In order for us to renew the policy coverage, you will have to submit an inspection report for the vessel. The inspection report usually requires you to produce all records of maintenance and prior inspections.

We will not be able to provide any insurance coverage without that inspection report.

 Very truly yours,

 Sheila Reynolds

 Sheila Reynolds

Exhibit 44

INSUR-ALL INSURANCE COMPANY

Memo to the File:
Dated: June 15, YR-2
From: Bob Richardson, Account manager

Mr. Fred Glenn, policy holder 890-938, called to report that his boat, The Riverboat Queen, had sunk in Beacon Lake. He said that there was no apparent cause for the boat to sink. There had not been any bad weather. There had not been any mechanical problems.

I asked Mr. Glenn when was the last time that the boat had been inspected, particularly the hull. He couldn't give me any date. I told him that it would be very important to determine what caused the boat to sink.

Mr. Glenn seemed to be very nervous, especially when I started questioning him about the hull and the different things that could have caused the boat to sink. I told him that he had to be certain that he used a recovery method that would best preserve the boat. I told him that the recovery company should try to float the boat up. I specifically told him that dragging the boat out might make it impossible to determine the cause of the boat sinking. At that point, he got really defensive—he may have detected that I was really skeptical because I had sent him a letter about a month ago telling him that we needed an inspection report in order to renew the policy. The policy would have expired on June 17.

A boat *mysteriously* sinking three days before the $500,000 policy expires—NOT LIKELY!

Exhibit 45

INSUR-ALL INSURANCE COMPANY

On June 15, YR-2, we received a phone call from Fred Glenn to report that his vessel, The Riverboat Queen, had mysteriously sunk in Beacon Lake. We have a policy on the vessel for $500,000. The policy would have expired at 5:00 p.m. on June 17, YR-2.

An inspection report was never produced by Mr. Glenn prior to our insuring the vessel. Somehow, this deficiency was not noted, and we issued the final binder providing full coverage. On May 17, YR-2, we sent Mr. Glenn a letter telling him that the policy would not be renewed unless he provided an inspection report. That letter was not returned to us. The next contact we had with Mr. Glenn was the aforementioned telephone call.

After the claim was referred to me, I reviewed our file. I then went to the boat ramp at Beacon Lake and spoke with Dolly Keith, one of the owners of Marine Rescue and Salvage (MRS), the company that had been hired to raise the boat. I told her who I was and explained my interest in trying to find out what caused the boat to sink. She told me that their divers had tried to feel around the boat to see if they could find any holes or breaks in the hull. She also said that the lake was very murky and that the divers had poor visibility. She said that she couldn't say for certain whether there were holes or not until the boat was brought up. She said that they were going to float the boat up so that they would not create any holes in the side of the boat. By floating it up, they would preserve the original damage to the boat. I asked her to call me when the boat was floated up.

I spoke to Ms. Keith when she called me. She told me that she was very frustrated with Mr. Glenn and that he kept interfering with their work. They were cutting the top off of the boat to make it lighter so they could float it up out of the water. She said that Mr. Glenn was now insisting that they just get bulldozers and drag the boat out. I told her that I was concerned that the boat would be so damaged from being dragged out that we would never be able to tell what had caused it to sink. She agreed.

The last time that I spoke with Ms. Keith was when she called to tell me that she had been fired. She said that Mr. Glenn was hiring a company that would use bulldozers to drag the boat out. She was convinced that Mr. Glenn had sunk the boat and was now going to try to conceal his actions by further damaging the boat.

Exhibit 46

November 10, YR-2

Insur-All Insurance Company
338 Main Street
Nita City, Nita 88890

      Re: *Policy #* 890-938

To Whom It May Concern:

Please allow this letter to confirm that I am making a claim for the total value of the Riverboat Queen that has been totally destroyed as a result of its sinking on June 14, YR-2, and being dragged from the lake. The total amount sought under this claim is $500,000. Please make the check payable to Fred Glenn.

                                  Thank you.

                                    Sincerely,

                                    Fred Glenn

Exhibit 47

November 18, YR-2

Mr. Fred Glenn
c/o Riverboat Queen
P.O. Box 123
Nita City, Nita 88888

     Re: *Insurance Claim*

Dear Mr. Glenn:

This will acknowledge receipt of your claim for payment of insurance proceeds under the insurance policy # 890-938. I regret to inform you that the claims bureau has determined that your claim should be denied. This decision is based on two considerations: 1) the absence of documents to establish that you properly maintained the vessel; 2) that there is a reasonable basis to believe that you contributed to the sinking of the Riverboat Queen.

We thank you for your business.

                    Sincerely,

                    Bob Richardson

Exhibit 48

From: lmurchison@nita.gov
Date: June 4, YR-2
To: Riverboat Queen riverboat@nita.com

Hey, Fred. You never responded to my e-mail. Are you getting the insurance renewed? Is there any kind of problem? It is really important that you get this done. Remember: no insurance = no lease. Please get in touch with me ASAP. It is urgent.

Exhibit 49

From: lmurchison@nita.gov
Date: May 20, YR-2
To: Riverboat Queen riverboat@nita.com

Hi Fred,

I was going through your file and noticed that your insurance policy expires on June 17. I know that you have a lot on your plate right now, so I wanted to make sure that you were on top of this. As you know, we have to have a copy of the policy in order to continue the lease. Please let me know that you are on top of this!

Linda

Exhibit 50

NITA CITY

Office of the City Manager
Nita City Hall
500 Main Street
Nita City, Nita 88888

December 3, YR-2

Mr. Fred Glenn
PO Box 123
Nita City, Nita 88888

Re: *Termination of lease*

Dear Mr. Glenn:

This letter is to notify you that your lease with Nita City for the boat ramp is hereby immediately terminated. The city invokes its rights under the provisions of the lease that require you to maintain insurance coverage. Additionally, the city invokes its rights to terminate the lease if it "reasonably believes" that you have engaged in unlawful activity. The city hereby notifies you that it reasonably believes that you have engaged in unlawful activity in that you attempted to defraud the Insur-All Insurance Company and created a risk of discharge of harmful pollutants into Beacon Lake.

Please remove all of your property from the boat dock within forty-eight (48) hours.

Truly yours,

Scott Gardner

Attachment: Lease between Nita City and Fred Glenn dba The Riverboat Queen

Exhibit 51

LEASE BETWEEN NITA CITY AND FRED GLENN DBA THE RIVERBOAT QUEEN

WHEREAS, Nita City (hereinafter "landlord") owns a boat ramp that is suitable for commercial use at Lake Nita;

WHEREAS, Fred Glenn, dba The Riverboat Queen, (hereinafter "Glenn") desires to use the boat ramp to operate The Riverboat Queen as an entertainment venue providing cruises, dinner, and special events,

WHEREAS, having The Riverboat Queen provide such activities for the residents of Nita City and surrounding environs will be a positive amenity to the services provided by Nita City,

IT IS HEREBY AGREED that Nita City shall lease to Glenn the boat ramp at Lake Nita for $2,000 a month beginning January 1, YR-3.

IT IS FURTHER UNDERSTOOD AND AGREED that because Nita City owns this boat ramp it is imperative that the business operations and conduct of The Riverboat Queen be above reproach and serve to further the reputation of Nita City. Accordingly, the landlord shall have the right to immediately terminate the lease if it reasonably believes that lessee has engaged in unlawful conduct.

IT IS FURTHER UNDERSTOOD AND AGREED that Glenn will maintain an insurance policy at all times for The Riverboat Queen during the term of this lease.

Fred Glenn

Fred Glenn dba The Riverboat Queen

Scott Gardner

Scott Gardner, City Manager

Exhibit 52

Memorandum: File
From: Bob Richardson
Re: Riverboat Queen and Fred Glenn

I went to the lake to look at The Riverboat Queen. I met Dolly Keith, who is in charge of the efforts to raise the boat. She was quite willing to talk about Fred Glenn, and it is pretty clear that she is very frustrated with this contract. Keith was quite critical of the Riverboat Queen, the way it was constructed, the absence of any detailed diagrams or plans. She said that Glenn initially seemed very concerned about getting the boat up in one piece, but that changed once they actually began the work to raise the boat. She also said that she overheard Glenn talking with his mechanic about the problems that he had, like the medical bills that he was getting from his wife's illness. She wasn't sure, but she thought the mechanic said something like "it'll be over soon when the insurance money comes in." Mr. Glenn said "yeah, luckiest thing that ever happened to me, the Riverboat Queen sinking when it did." She said that Mr. Glenn was laughing when he said that.

Jury Instructions

Breach of Contract

For a contract to be valid, there must be an offer and an acceptance of that offer. An acceptance is a statement or conduct that shows that a person agrees to all of the terms of the offer and intends to be bound by them.

The parties to a contract can agree to modify a contract. Whether the contract was modified by the parties depends on their intent as shown by the words, whether written or oral, or their conduct.

You will decide the meaning of contested terms of the contract. You must decide what the intent of the parties was when the contract was made. You should look to the language of the contract. You may also consider the circumstances under which the parties made the contract, and what the parties themselves believed the terms meant as shown by the evidence.

A contract is to be interpreted as a whole, and the overall intention of the parties is controlling over the separate parts of a contract. Each part of a contract must be used to help interpret the other parts, but if one part is wholly inconsistent with the general intention of the parties, it should be rejected.

By agreeing to perform work in a contract, a person promises to use reasonable skill, care, and diligence and that the work will be done in a workmanlike manner and be reasonably fit for its intended use.

A contract is breached when a party does not do what he/she/it promised to do in the contract.

A party is not required to perform each and every term of a contract completely and exactly to recover for the breach. A party who has substantially performed a contract is entitled to recover. Performance is substantial when most of the work required has been performed, any remaining work or errors can be easily completed, and the contracting party was acting in good faith towards completion of the contract.

A contract is breached when one party notifies the other party that that party does not intend to do as promised in the contract. It is not a breach of a contract if a party merely complains about the contract or expresses doubt about whether to do what was promised.

A party is relieved of the duty to perform a contract if the other party to the contract prevented that party from performing.

A party is relieved of the duty to perform a contract if:

1) The other party to the contract prevented the performance;

2) The other party to the contract voluntarily and intentionally gave up the right to require performance of the contract; or

3) The other party, by acts or conduct, indicated intent not to enforce the contract so that a reasonable person would think that performance of the contract was no longer required.

A contract may provide that the duty of one party to perform does not arise until after the performance of some act or the happening of some event this is known as a condition precedent. To decide whether or not certain action is a condition precedent to the duty to perform, you must decide what the parties intended. To do so, you may consider the language of the contract, the circumstances under which parties made the contract, and what the parties themselves believed as shown by the evidence.

Jury Instructions

Fraud

Fraud relieves a party of the duty to perform a contract. Fraud includes any statement or act that is intended to deceive another party to influence that party to enter into the contract. In addition, the party must have relied on the fraudulent statement or act in entering into the contract. Fraud consists of:

1) A suggestion, as a fact, of something that is not true, when the person making the suggestion does not believe it to be the truth; or

2) A positive statement of something that is not true, when the person making it had no reasonable basis for the statement; or

3) A person's concealment of something that he knows is the truth; or

4) A promise made without any intention of performing it; or

5) A person remaining silent when he had a duty to speak. [Plaintiff] had a duty to tell [Defendant] about [the information that was not disclosed] because [give the specific reason for this duty of disclosure]; or

6) Any other statement [or act] intended to deceive.

Fraud must be proven by clear and convincing evidence. This means you must be persuaded, considering all the evidence in the case, it is highly probable and free from serious doubt that the contract was obtained through fraud.

Jury Instructions

General Measure of Damages

If you decide for one of the parties on the claim for breach of contract, you must then fix the amount of the damages. This is the amount of money that is needed to put the party in as good a position as that party would have been if the contract had not been breached. The amount of damages does not have to be proved with mathematical certainty, but there must be a reasonable basis for the award.

Jury Instructions

Insurance Claim

An insurance company has a duty to deal fairly and act in good faith with the Insurer. There is a claim that the Insurer violated its duty of good faith and fair dealing by unreasonably, and in bad faith, refusing to pay the proper amount for a valid claim under the insurance policy. For damages to be recovered in this case, the greater weight of the evidence must show that:

1. The Insurer was required under the insurance policy to pay the claim;

2. The Insurer's refusal to pay the claim in full was unreasonable under the circumstances because

    a) It did not perform a proper investigation; or

    b) It did not evaluate the results of the investigation properly; or

    c) It had no reasonable basis for the refusal.

Jury Instructions

Bad Faith—Damages

If you find that the Insurer violated its duty of good faith and fair dealing, you must fix the amount of Plaintiff's damages. This is the amount of money that will compensate [him/her/it] for any loss suffered as a result of the Insurer's failure to pay Plaintiff's claim. In fixing the amount you will award Plaintiff you may consider the following elements:

1. Financial losses;

2. Embarrassment and loss of reputation; and

3. Mental pain and suffering.

JURY INSTRUCTIONS

NITA WATER HAZARD ACT

The Nita Water Hazard Act provides: "whoever shall knowingly or recklessly cause any condition that leads or could lead to a discharge of pollutants into waters of the state, shall be subject to imprisonment for a term not to exceed three years and a fine not to exceed $100,000." Knowingly shall mean with purpose or deliberation that a condition be created that would lead or could lead to a discharge of pollutants. Recklessly shall mean that the individual knew that their actions could cause a condition that would or could lead to a discharge of pollutants into waters of the state but decided to engage in the conduct. It is a defense to a prosecution under this statute that the defendant used reasonable and customary care in its disposal of hazardous materials.

Beacon Lake is a lake owned by the State of Nita.

Jury Instructions

Attempted Insurance Fraud

Section 42.5 of Nita Criminal Code provides that whoever, with intent to defraud or deceive an insurer, the person, in support of a claim for payment under an insurance policy, knowingly makes a statement that contains false or misleading material information shall be guilty of an offense and subject to punishment not to exceed five years imprisonment.

You are hereby instructed that a "claim for payment" needs not be on any specific form. A letter can be a claim. "Material information" is information of such a nature that it would influence a decision-maker.